How to Overcome Fear and Anxiety

Crafted by Skriuwer

Copyright © 2024 by Skriuwer.

All rights reserved. No part of this book may be used or reproduced in any form whatsoever without written permission except in the case of brief quotations in critical articles or reviews.

For more information, contact : **kontakt@skriuwer.com** (www.skriuwer.com)

TABLE OF CONTENTS

Chapter 1: Facing Fear: A Basic View
1.1 Introduction
1.2 What Fear Really Is
1.3 Common Signs and Triggers
1.4 Key Steps to Begin Managing Fear

Chapter 2: The Nature of Anxiety: Getting to the Heart of It
2.1 Defining Anxiety
2.2 Why It Grows Over Time
2.3 Spotting Daily Anxiety Clues
2.4 Linking Fear and Anxiety

Chapter 3: Thoughts and Feelings: How They Shape Our Reactions
3.1 The Loop of Thoughts and Emotions
3.2 Recognizing Negative Thought Patterns
3.3 Early Methods to Ease Worry
3.4 Shifting Our Inner Voice

Chapter 4: Outside Factors That Feed Fear and Anxiety
4.1 Social Pressures and Daily Tension
4.2 The Role of Media and Technology
4.3 Stressful Events and Change
4.4 Setting Boundaries to Reduce Overload

Chapter 5: Ways to Calm Tension and Stress
5.1 Slow Breathing and Grounding
5.2 Simple Relaxation Methods
5.3 Focusing Attention Wisely
5.4 Quick Stress Relief Tools

Chapter 6: Using Steady Routines for Inner Peace

6.1 Why Routines Protect Against Anxiety
6.2 Morning and Evening Rituals
6.3 Balancing Activity and Rest
6.4 Making Routines Work for You

Chapter 7: Techniques for a More Peaceful Mind

7.1 Automatic Thoughts and How to Spot Them
7.2 Common Distortions That Fuel Fear
7.3 Reframing Negative Ideas
7.4 Acceptance Instead of Fighting Thoughts

Chapter 8: Building Inner Strength

8.1 Self-Worth and Fear
8.2 Trusting Yourself in Difficult Times
8.3 Creating a Sense of Purpose
8.4 Growing Resilience Step by Step

Chapter 9: Steps to Slow Down Panic

9.1 Understanding the Panic Cycle
9.2 Grounding and Breathing During Panic
9.3 Changing Fearful Predictions
9.4 Gradual Exposure to Key Triggers

Chapter 10: Handling Pressure in Daily Living

10.1 Recognizing Hidden Daily Strains
10.2 Sorting and Prioritizing Tasks
10.3 Micro-Breaks for Quick Stress Control
10.4 Keeping a Long-View Outlook

Chapter 11: Finding the Right Support System

11.1 Types of Helpful Support
11.2 Identifying True Helpers
11.3 Communicating Your Needs
11.4 Building a Network That Sustains You

Chapter 12: Challenging Unhelpful Thoughts
12.1 Spotting Distorted Thinking
12.2 Using Thought Records Effectively
12.3 Replacing Harsh Labels with Balanced Views
12.4 Sustaining the Shift in Mindset

Chapter 13: The Power of Self-Talk
13.1 Negative Self-Talk Patterns
13.2 Building a Kinder Inner Voice
13.3 Handling Self-Doubt
13.4 Making the Coach Voice Stronger

Chapter 14: Turning Stress into a Helpful Force
14.1 Understanding Good vs. Bad Stress
14.2 The "Flow Zone" and Growth
14.3 Reframing Stress at Work or School
14.4 Preventing Burnout Over Time

Chapter 15: Facing Fear in Public Spaces
15.1 Handling Crowds and Confined Areas
15.2 Steady Steps for Speaking in Groups
15.3 Setting Boundaries in Social Events
15.4 Tools for Staying Calm on the Spot

Chapter 16: Keeping Balance Between Work and Personal Life
16.1 Signs of Imbalance and How They Grow Anxiety
16.2 Setting Clear Boundaries and Limits
16.3 Planning Days for Steady Momentum
16.4 Building a Supportive Home and Work Routine

Chapter 17: Coping with Setbacks and Slips
17.1 Why Setbacks Happen
17.2 Early Clues Before a Full Slip
17.3 Self-Compassion During a Slip
17.4 Learning from Each Setback

Chapter 18: Making Purposeful Changes
18.1 Spotting Habits That Need Shifts
18.2 Setting Clear Goals and Plans
18.3 Staying Flexible and Adjusting
18.4 Tracking Progress and Celebrating Wins

Chapter 19: Keeping the Body Strong for Less Anxiety
19.1 Movement and Tension Release
19.2 The Role of Sleep and Nutrition
19.3 Calmer Breathing Habits
19.4 Balancing Activity and Rest

Chapter 20: Hope for a Bright Tomorrow
20.1 Why Hope Weakens Fear
20.2 Finding Good Moments and Purpose
20.3 Holding Onto Optimism in Hard Times
20.4 Bringing It All Together

PART ONE: BUILDING A BASE

CHAPTER 1: FACING FEAR: A BASIC VIEW

Introduction

Fear is a strong feeling that can take hold of our thoughts and bodies in many ways. It can keep us awake at night, or it can push us to do things we thought we could not do. It is easy to think that fear is simply about threats or dangers around us, but there is more to it than that. Fear also has a way of working in our minds, causing us to worry about what may happen. It can show up in small parts of our day, or it can appear in a major way when we least expect it.

Many people think fear is always bad. That is not true. Fear can alert us when something is not right. It can help us avoid harm, like stepping away from a dangerous animal. It can also help us plan wisely, like double-checking our seat belt before driving. But problems with fear start when it does not go away. It can turn into a heavy burden that weighs us down. It can keep us from trying new things because we are scared of failing. It can keep us from speaking up when we have an idea, in case people laugh at us. When fear takes over, it can block us from living fully.

In this chapter, we will look at what fear really is. We will talk about how it shows up in the mind and body. We will also look at how it shapes our habits and day-to-day choices. By looking at these basic ideas, we can build a path toward handling fear in a calmer way. The goal is to make sense of it, not to remove it from life fully. Instead, we want to learn to keep it in check so we can stay focused on what matters to us.

What Is Fear?

Fear starts as a reaction to a threat. That threat can be real, like a wild dog on the street, or it can be in our thoughts, like the idea that we may fail an exam. In both cases, our body and mind respond in similar ways. Our heart might beat faster, we might start to sweat, and our breath may become short or shallow. These things happen because our system is preparing us to face or escape from danger.

The basic pathway of fear often involves a small part of the brain called the amygdala. When we see or sense a threat, the amygdala signals the rest of the brain and body. It says, "Get ready for action!" Hormones like adrenaline can then surge through the body. This causes the well-known signs: fast heartbeat, tense muscles, and more alert senses. When we are in real danger, this reaction is a helpful tool. It can mean the difference between safety and harm.

Trouble arises when the same reaction stays active or flares up for situations that are not truly harmful. For example, a person might feel the same rush of fear at the thought of speaking in front of a group. The body acts like the person is in physical danger, which can make daily events feel overwhelming. That is one way fear can turn from a good warning sign into a constant chain around the person's life.

How Fear Can Grow Over Time

Fear can become bigger in our thoughts without us noticing it. One way this happens is called "avoidance." A person who feels fear in social settings might start to skip meeting friends or speaking in a group. This might seem like a quick fix. By avoiding the scary event, the person does not have to feel that strong wave of fear. But over time, avoidance only makes fear stronger. It keeps us from learning that we can handle the event. It also prevents us from practicing ways to reduce our fear in that moment.

Another way fear can grow is through "what-if" thinking. We might ask ourselves, "What if I make a mistake?" or "What if I look foolish?" These thoughts can spin out of control. If we keep asking "What if?" in a negative way, we might start to believe the worst outcomes. Then fear takes root. We end up missing out on chances to learn and connect with others.

Over time, these habits can shape our daily life. We might pick safe paths in our work, not taking on new tasks because we are worried. We might limit our social life, picking only the groups or places where we feel less at risk of being judged. This might feel nice and calm at first, but our world can become smaller. The sense of calm is also built on avoiding fear, not dealing with it head-on.

Common Forms of Fear

1. Fear of failure: This can show up when we do not want to look bad in front of others. We might stay away from new duties or tasks because the idea of failing is too scary. This fear can stop our growth, as we never test our limits or find out what we can learn from mistakes.
2. Fear of rejection: Many people feel this when they think of speaking their mind. We worry that others might not like what we have to say. We might not raise our hand in class or speak at meetings. We might keep quiet with friends or family. Over time, we can start to feel alone because we do not share our thoughts.
3. Fear of the unknown: This can appear when we face big changes or new places. For instance, moving to a new city or starting a new job can spark fear. The unknown can feel huge. We do not know how things will turn out, so our mind fills in the gaps with the worst images. As a result, we might miss out on new paths that could help us grow or find joy.
4. Fear of conflict: Some people feel worried about any type of argument or disagreement. They might hold back their true feelings for peace. But never speaking up can make problems grow. It can also create hidden stress that harms personal ties.

These forms of fear can mix together. For example, a person might fear failure and also fear conflict, which might mean they avoid tasks and also avoid speaking with their boss or friends about problems. This can build up over time, making them feel stuck.

The Link Between Fear and the Body

Fear has a direct effect on the body. When we sense something scary, our system goes into a "fight or flight" mode. This can mean:

- **Fast heartbeat**: Our heart pumps more blood to our muscles so we can move or defend ourselves.
- **Shallow breathing**: The body tries to get oxygen faster. This can lead to shortness of breath or that feeling of being "on edge."
- **Tense muscles**: The body tightens in case it needs to run or fight.
- **Sweating**: Our system tries to cool down in case we have to move quickly.

These reactions are not harmful if they happen for a short time. But if fear becomes an everyday thing, these signs can harm our health. Chronic tension can lead to muscle pain. Fast heartbeat over a long period can put extra pressure on the heart. Shortness of breath can affect how we function day to day.

The mind and body also interact in a loop. When the body shows fear signs, the mind might pick up on them and think, "I must be in danger." Then it sends more danger signals back to the body. Breaking this loop can be a key step in handling fear. If we can steady our breathing, our mind might calm down. If we can remind ourselves that the danger might not be real, our heartbeat might slow.

First Steps to Facing Fear

Before we can handle fear, we need to accept that it exists. This does not mean we have to like it. It only means we need to see that fear is part of our human makeup. We cannot make it vanish by force. But we can work on how we react when fear appears.

One first step is to **name** it. We can say to ourselves, "I feel fear right now." That small action can help us see that fear is an emotion, not a fact about who we are. It helps create a gap between ourselves and the feeling. Now we can look at it, rather than being lost in it.

Another step is to check the facts. If we are worried about what people think of us, we can ask ourselves if there is real proof that something bad will happen. This does not always remove fear, but it can take away some of the intensity. It helps us see that we might be making a problem bigger in our mind than it is in real life.

We can also learn small **calming** methods, such as steady breathing. For example, we can breathe in for a count of four, hold for a brief moment, and breathe out for a count of four. Doing this a few times can slow the heart rate and send a note to the mind that we are safe right now.

Impact of Fear on Our Minds

Fear can limit our actions. It can make us cautious about things that do not pose real danger. When fear is not managed, it can change how we see ourselves and our world. We might think in terms of worst-case outcomes. We might label ourselves as timid or unable to cope. This can cause us to give up on many dreams or plans.

Fear can also cloud our judgment. We might react too fast or pick poor solutions because we want to escape the fear. In that rush, we might make decisions based on what feels safe, rather than what might be good for us in the long run. This can lead to regrets later.

The way fear appears in our thoughts can take several forms:

- **Catastrophic thinking**: This is when our mind leaps to the worst possible scenario.
- **Overgeneralizing**: If one bad thing happens, we might think it will always happen in every case.
- **Black-and-white thinking**: We might see everything as either perfect or a complete failure.

These patterns can keep us stuck. But the good news is that we can learn to change them with patience and careful effort.

Shifting How We See Fear

Learning about fear is the first step to handling it in a healthier way. Instead of trying to push it away, we can look at why it appears. Is it based on a real threat or a learned response? If it is a learned response, can we start to unlearn it? If it is a real threat, can we manage it wisely?

We can also remind ourselves that fear, by itself, is not our enemy. It is a natural sign from our body and mind that we need to pay attention to something. But we get to choose what to do with that sign. Will we let fear run our day, or will we note the fear and then take a calmer path?

As we go through this book, we will learn ways to face fear without letting it control us. We will learn to reduce its power in our minds and in our daily life.

This does not happen in one day. It is a process, and it requires patience. But every bit of progress, no matter how small, can open up more room in our lives to grow and do the things that matter to us.

Fear as a Building Block

It may sound odd, but fear can even help us learn about ourselves. If we look at what we fear, we can discover what we care about. If we are scared of failing, it may mean we care about success or respect. If we fear rejection, it may mean we care about being liked or loved. Recognizing these things can help us see what is truly important. Then we can find ways to work on those goals more directly, rather than letting fear lock us up.

Conclusion of Chapter 1

Fear is not simple. It has mental, physical, and social parts. It can guide us to act in times of real danger, or it can hold us back when we let it grow too strong. By learning its roots and how it appears, we begin to set the stage for handling it well. In the next chapter, we will look at **anxiety**, which often goes hand in hand with fear. We will see how anxiety can spin thoughts and heighten feelings until they become hard to manage. And we will start to explore what steps we can take to ease that anxious grip on our minds.

CHAPTER 2: THE NATURE OF ANXIETY: GETTING TO THE HEART OF IT

Introduction

Anxiety is closely tied to fear, but it has its own shape. While fear often arises in response to a real or clear threat, anxiety can show up without an obvious cause. It can linger in the background or strike us in a sudden wave. Anxiety can leave us feeling edgy, tense, or even shaky. For some people, it is a low-level hum that never goes away. For others, it arrives in bursts, like panic attacks.

Learning about anxiety in depth can help us see what it is and why it grows. We can discover how it affects our thoughts, bodies, and choices. We can also begin to notice ways to reduce it. In this chapter, we will talk about the meaning of anxiety, how it develops, and how it can shape our life. We will also look at ways we might slowly break its hold on us.

What Is Anxiety?

Anxiety is a state of nervousness or worry about what might happen in the future. Unlike fear, which is often tied to a real threat in the present, anxiety can focus on possibilities rather than facts. It might stem from a range of worries: health, finances, social acceptance, or anything else that matters to us.

Our body's response to anxiety can be similar to the fear response. We may feel our heart race or notice shallow breathing. We might feel our stomach churn or get a sense of tightness in the chest. Anxiety can also affect our sleep, appetite, and ability to focus. When anxiety becomes a regular part of life, it can lead to ongoing stress and wear us down.

Different Types of Anxiety

Anxiety does not look the same for everyone. Some may have generalized anxiety, where they worry about many areas of life. Others might have social anxiety, which focuses on how people see them. Some might have panic attacks that strike quickly, making them feel like they cannot breathe or that they are losing control. Still others may have worries limited to one type of situation, such as fear of flying.

The details can vary, but a common thread is a sense of dread about what could go wrong. This dread can cause us to keep our guard up. We might second-guess ourselves a lot, searching for any sign that something bad is about to happen. Over time, this constant state of watchfulness can strain both our mind and body.

Why Anxiety Grows and Lingers

Anxiety often has roots in our biology and our upbringing. Some people are more prone to anxiety due to their genes. They may have a more active stress response. Others might learn anxious patterns from parents or caregivers who were also tense and worried. There can be real-life events that plant seeds of anxiety, such as a frightening experience at school or in public. Later, the mind starts to see danger everywhere, even if the danger is not present anymore.

Anxiety is also fed by the habit of **rumination**. This is when we go over our worries again and again in our heads. We might try to solve them mentally, but we only get stuck in a loop of negative thoughts. Each time we circle back to the same worry, we feel more stressed. Our body can respond as though the threat is real and current.

Avoidance makes anxiety worse too. When we avoid something that scares us, we do not get the chance to test our fears. We never learn that we can handle the situation. This lack of practice keeps the anxiety strong. It also gives us the short-term relief of not facing the fear, which teaches our brain that avoidance is a quick fix. The next time anxiety shows up, we will likely avoid the trigger again, reinforcing the pattern.

Signs and Symptoms of Anxiety

Anxiety can show up in many ways, from mental signs to physical feelings. Here are some common ones:

- **Excessive worry**: Feeling on edge or nervous about many things.
- **Restlessness**: Feeling like we cannot sit still or relax.
- **Trouble sleeping**: Either trouble falling asleep or staying asleep.

- **Fatigue**: Worry can use up energy, leaving us tired.
- **Irritability**: Feeling annoyed or losing our temper easily.
- **Concentration problems**: Hard to focus or remember tasks.
- **Muscle tension**: Shoulders, neck, and back might ache.

Not everyone will have all these signs. Some might only have one or two. But if these signs are strong or long-lasting, they might point to an anxiety problem. Recognizing them is the first step to handling them.

The Role of Thoughts in Anxiety

Anxiety can stem from how we think about ourselves and the world. If we always expect the worst, our body reacts with tense feelings. If we keep replaying embarrassing moments in our head, we teach ourselves that these moments are huge and define who we are. If we assume people are judging us, we might fear social events without proof that this is true.

Negative thought habits often play a big role here. We might jump to conclusions, thinking that one awkward moment at a party means no one liked us. We might blow problems out of proportion, seeing a small setback as a sign of total failure. We might also label ourselves with negative terms like "weak" or "useless," which keeps anxiety strong.

The Physical Cycle of Anxiety

When we feel anxious, our system responds as if we are in danger. Our body pumps out stress hormones, our heart beats faster, and our senses stay on alert. This is not a problem if it happens once in a while. But if it happens daily or even several times a day, our body never fully calms down. This can lead to chronic stress, which might impact our immune system, digestion, and heart health over time.

There is also a feedback loop. Our anxious thoughts tell our body to tense up, and when we feel that tension, we think, "Yes, I must be in danger," which leads to more anxious thoughts. Breaking this loop can involve calming the body. By learning to breathe more slowly or relax our muscles, we can send a new message to our mind. Over time, this can lessen the anxious reaction.

Anxiety vs. Fear

Fear and anxiety are close relatives. They often overlap, but they are not the same. Fear is usually tied to a real threat or situation happening now. Anxiety is often linked to things that might happen or things we imagine could happen. Anxiety can linger before and after an event, creating a sense of dread that does not let up.

Still, these two states often feed each other. If we fear a certain situation, we might have anxiety about it days or weeks before it even occurs. Once we face the situation, the fear might spike. Then, after it is over, we might worry about how it went, replaying it in our mind. This cycle can continue, growing in intensity unless we find ways to step in and guide our thoughts in a calmer direction.

How Anxiety Can Shape Our Lives

When anxiety grows strong, it can change our routine. We might stop doing things we once liked. We might stay home more because going out feels too overwhelming. We might avoid calls or messages from friends because we fear bad news. Over time, this can cause our world to shrink. We might have fewer ties to other people. Our health might suffer if we avoid doctor visits due to anxiety. Our work or school performance might drop if we freeze up in front of tasks or tests.

Anxiety can also strain our close ties. We might need constant reassurance, or we might withdraw to avoid people seeing our worry. We might ask loved ones to keep everything "safe" for us, limiting their freedom as well. This can cause conflict, confusion, and sadness for everyone involved.

The good news is that anxiety is not a life sentence. It is a learned set of reactions that can be changed. With the right mindset and some new tools, we can reduce anxiety's power and take back control over our choices.

The Link Between Anxiety and Mood

Anxiety can affect our mood in big ways. Constant worry or tension can lead to sadness or loss of hope. Feeling like we cannot relax or enjoy life can feed into low mood. It might also push us into a sense of helplessness, where we think we cannot fix our problems. This can become a circle: anxiety sparks a drop in mood, which in turn makes us more prone to anxious thoughts.

Breaking this cycle may involve caring for our overall emotional health. That can include taking time for rest, learning to talk kindly to ourselves, and seeking help when needed. It is common for anxiety and low mood to appear together, so handling both might be part of the process.

First Steps to Handle Anxiety

One helpful step is to **notice** when anxious thoughts come up. We do not have to force these thoughts away, but we can label them: "Here is an anxious thought." By naming it, we remind ourselves that it is just a thought, not a fact. We can then decide how much attention to give it.

Practicing slow and steady **breathing** can also help. When we feel anxiety rising, we can pause. We can breathe in through our nose for a count of four, hold for a brief count, and breathe out through our mouth for four counts. Doing this a few times may lower our heart rate and help the body shift out of panic mode.

It is also helpful to place some limits on worry time. For instance, we can set aside 10 or 15 minutes a day to think about our worries. When anxious thoughts pop up outside that time, we can say, "I will focus on that later, during worry time." This can take practice, but it helps train the mind not to dwell on worries all day.

Looking Ahead: Combining Tools

In later parts of this book, we will explore many ways to handle anxiety. We will look at how to change our thought patterns, how to calm the body, and how to take small steps toward the things we fear. We will also talk about how to seek help from others, including friends, family, or professionals.

Our aim is to guide our minds away from constant worry and panic toward a calmer and clearer outlook. This does not mean anxiety or fear will vanish forever. But it does mean we can learn to keep them in check. We can see them without letting them rule our actions.

Why This Foundation Matters

Fear and anxiety can feel very different for each person. But the basics we covered in these first two chapters set up the rest of our path. We have seen that fear and anxiety are natural, but they can become big obstacles if we do not manage them. We have looked at how they show up in our bodies and thoughts. We have also seen how they can shape our day-to-day life and even affect the people around us.

Understanding these basics can help us as we move on to the next parts of the book. We will begin to dig into specific triggers, daily skills, thought patterns, and actions that can reduce the hold fear and anxiety have on us. The more we know about where these feelings come from, the easier it becomes to meet them head-on with steady steps.

Conclusion of Chapter 2

Anxiety can show up in many forms, but at its core, it is an overactive worry about the future or about events that might not happen. It can grow through habits like avoidance and negative thinking. It can also lock us into a cycle of stress that affects both our mind and body. The important thing to remember is that anxiety, like fear, is a normal reaction that can get out of hand. By learning to spot it and using simple methods to slow it down, we can start to change its course.

In the next part of our book, we will explore triggers for fear and anxiety and look at the first steps to deal with them. We will also see how our thoughts and feelings shape our actions, and how outside factors can add to our worries. This will help us gain a broader view of where fear and anxiety come from, giving us the knowledge to begin shifting our actions in a strong and steady way.

PART TWO: TRIGGERS AND FIRST STEPS

The pages that follow continue our path toward handling **fear** and **anxiety**. Part Two will focus on the triggers that set off these strong emotions, as well as the first steps to work through them. We will look at how our thoughts and feelings shape our reactions, and then we will turn our attention to the outside factors that can feed these inner storms. By the end of these two chapters, you will have a clearer idea of how triggers arise and what small actions you can take to begin steady change.

CHAPTER 3: THOUGHTS AND FEELINGS: HOW THEY SHAPE OUR REACTIONS

Introduction

Most of us know what it feels like when our mind races with worry. We might sense our heart pumping hard, notice our stomach clenching, or feel our hands get clammy. These signs come from the link between our **thoughts**, **feelings**, and bodily reactions. When fear or anxiety sets in, it does not only live in our heads. It changes how our body acts and how we feel about ourselves.

This chapter looks at why this happens. We will explore how our thoughts affect what we feel and do, and how those feelings can, in turn, fuel more thoughts and reactions. By understanding this cycle, we can learn to spot triggers more quickly and begin to replace old habits with new responses that bring calm.

The Impact of Thoughts on Fear and Anxiety

A key idea in dealing with fear and anxiety is the power of our thoughts. We often assume our worries come directly from an outside cause. While certain events can spark fear, our interpretation of those events is what truly shapes how we feel. For instance, if you get a new work task and your first thought is, "I will fail," you may feel a wave of dread. If another person sees the same task and thinks, "I can handle this if I plan carefully," they may feel more at ease.

Our minds have a constant inner voice that comments on what is happening. This voice can be negative, neutral, or positive. When our inner voice leans toward negative ideas, fear and anxiety can grow. If we learn to guide our thoughts toward more realistic or balanced ones, we can often reduce the strength of anxious feelings. This does not mean we have to force ourselves to be overly positive. It means learning to see the full picture without jumping to the worst conclusions.

The Loop of Thoughts, Feelings, and Actions

We can think of a three-part loop. First, something happens around or inside us (a trigger). Then we have a thought about that trigger. That thought sparks a feeling, such as fear, anxiety, or panic. Then that feeling often pushes us toward an action, like running away, freezing up, or avoiding the situation in the future.

After that action, our mind judges what happened. If we ran away from the trigger, our mind might confirm that the event was "too scary to handle." That judgment then feeds back into our next round of thoughts, making it more likely that the cycle repeats. Over time, if we do not interrupt the cycle, it can become a habit.

By learning about this loop, we can see that changing our thoughts can shift our feelings. Changing how we feel can shift what we do. And changing what we do can alter our beliefs about the event. Each of these parts affects the other, so a small change in one area can set off big improvements across the board.

Emotional Triggers: Where Do They Come From?

Triggers can be many things: a place, a memory, a smell, a person's tone of voice, or even a quick thought that drifts across our mind. Sometimes triggers come from past experiences we have not fully processed. If we once had an embarrassing moment in a crowded room, the thought of going to a busy place might set off anxiety.

Triggers can also come from small daily frustrations. Let's say you are stuck in traffic and worry you will be late for an appointment. That stress might spark a memory of other times you were late and got in trouble. Soon your mind might jump to thoughts like, "I always mess up," which leads to more anxious feelings.

When we look closer at triggers, we often see patterns. These patterns help us notice how our mind moves from one thought to another. By spotting these patterns, we can begin to predict when a trigger might appear, making it easier to prepare ourselves with calming methods.

The Role of Feelings in This Cycle

Feelings come after thoughts, but they can also appear quickly and powerfully. Sometimes it can seem as though the feeling happens first, and then the thought. But in most cases, a spark of thought, even if tiny, sets off the wave of emotion.

For example, you might walk into a meeting and suddenly feel uneasy. Before you can pin down why, your chest tightens. On closer examination, you might find that the cause is a flash of thought: "What if they ask me questions I cannot answer?" This thought is so fast you barely catch it. Yet it lights up your body's stress reaction.

Feelings are not under direct control, which can make them scary. You cannot just press a button and remove the feeling of fear. But you can learn to guide it by changing the thoughts that fuel it. When the mind is telling a fearful story, the body will often respond in fearful ways.

Why Some Thoughts Are Hard to Shake

Certain thoughts hold more power because of past experiences or beliefs we grew up with. If you were criticized a lot as a child, you might hold onto a core thought that says, "I am not good enough." This belief can pop up in many places: at work, in relationships, even when facing personal goals. Each time you approach a challenge, that belief might whisper, "You will fail," which sparks fear or anxiety.

Also, repeated emotional experiences can set up strong memory links in the brain. Let's say you once froze up when speaking in front of a group at school.

Now, any hint of public speaking can bring back that memory. The feeling arises, and you might react the same way: with trembling hands, shortness of breath, and a wish to avoid the situation.

These deep patterns do not vanish by ignoring them. The first step is to notice them. Sometimes it helps to write down the most common negative thoughts. By putting them on paper, we see them more clearly. Then we can question them.

Questioning Negative Thoughts

One simple but powerful tool is to ask, "Is this thought true?" For instance, if the thought is "I always fail," we can step back and see if that is fact. Are there times when we did not fail? If so, the thought might be an exaggeration.

Another question is, "Is there any proof for or against this thought?" We might find that the mind is picking out only the bad moments and forgetting the good. We might recall times we succeeded or times we found a decent result, even if not perfect.

We can also ask, "What is the worst thing that can happen if this thought is correct, and how would I deal with it?" Often, our greatest fear is that we would not cope. But in many cases, we could find a way to get through it, even if it was tough or uncomfortable.

By questioning our thoughts, we weaken their hold on us. We might still feel anxious, but we can chip away at the idea that the thought must be true. Over time, this can allow us to form more balanced ways of seeing ourselves and the world.

Feelings of Shame and Guilt as Triggers

Shame and guilt can be powerful triggers for fear and anxiety. Shame is the sense that we are flawed or unworthy, while guilt is the feeling that we did something wrong. Both can lead us to expect negative outcomes. If we feel shame, we might think, "I do not deserve good things," which sparks fear when good opportunities appear. If we feel guilt, we might think, "I will be punished," which can cause us to stay on edge and worry.

Sometimes shame and guilt have clear reasons, such as a mistake we made in the past. Other times, they come from negative messages we received that were not fair or accurate. Either way, these feelings can fuel anxiety if we do not address them. We might avoid situations that bring them to the surface, limiting our life in the process.

Physical Sensations as Warnings

Our body often reacts to fearful thoughts before our conscious mind registers them. A chill down the spine, a sudden drop in the stomach, or a rush of heat in the face might be an early sign that we feel threatened. Recognizing these signs can help us pause and notice what is happening.

If we learn to spot these bodily signals, we have a chance to step back and ask, "What thought passed through my mind just now?" or "Why am I feeling this sudden shift?" This small gap can stop the surge of anxiety from taking full control. It gives us time to use a calming strategy.

Practical Steps to Shift the Inner Dialogue

1. **Identify the thought**: Whenever you feel a sudden wave of fear, try to label the thought that sparked it.
2. **Ask if it is accurate**: Check if the thought is based on facts or on assumptions.
3. **Consider other views**: Think of at least one other way to see the situation that does not lead to the worst outcome.
4. **Try a calming method**: Take slow breaths, relax your shoulders, or place a hand on your chest to remind yourself you are safe in this moment.

Even a brief pause to do this can weaken the fear response. It might not remove all anxiety, but it can cut down how much it grows. Doing this again and again over time builds a healthier habit.

Why Changing Thoughts Takes Time

Our thoughts are shaped by years of habits, upbringing, and experiences. We should not expect to change them overnight. There can be setbacks. We might be able to catch and question our thoughts one day, but slip back into old patterns the next. That does not mean we failed. It is part of the process.

Every time we notice a negative thought and question it, we are strengthening new pathways in the brain. These new pathways will feel weak at first, but with practice, they become stronger. Bit by bit, the old paths of worry and fear can fade.

Emotions vs. Reason: Finding Balance

Some people think they must use logic to beat emotions. Others believe they should follow their heart all the time. In truth, both reason and emotion matter. Emotions give us signals about our inner state, while logic can help us check if those signals are accurate.

If we rely only on logic, we might overlook important feelings that tell us something is wrong. If we rely only on feelings, we might miss important facts that show we are safer than we think. Learning to balance both is key.

The Power of Naming Emotions

When fear or anxiety strikes, it might feel like a huge wave we cannot define. Naming the emotion can help us see it clearly. We can say, "I feel **worried**," or "I feel **afraid**," or "I feel **uncertain**." By putting a word to it, we separate the emotion from ourselves. We see that it is an experience, not who we are.

Naming the emotion can also help guide us to the next step. If it is worry, maybe we need to set aside time for problem-solving. If it is fear, perhaps we need to remind ourselves that the danger might not be real. If it is uncertainty, we could explore ways to accept that life has unknowns we cannot fully control.

Inner Speech and Self-Talk

Many of us speak to ourselves in a tone we would never use with others. We might call ourselves names or harshly criticize small mistakes. This kind of self-talk can keep us trapped in fear. We end up seeing ourselves as lacking or unable to handle life.

Changing our self-talk does not mean we have to say things we do not believe. It can mean speaking to ourselves like a friend would: calmly and honestly. Instead of saying, "I am useless," we could say, "I am having a hard time right now, but I can do small steps to get through it." This does not have to be flowery or forced. Simple, kind words to ourselves can make a big difference in how we feel.

Emotional Resilience: Building a Gradual Defense

When our thoughts shift from negative to more realistic, we slowly gain what some call emotional resilience. This does not mean we do not feel fear or anxiety. It means we can bounce back more quickly. We can face a trigger, feel the spark of worry, and then calm ourselves before it grows too large.

Resilience grows as we prove to ourselves that we can handle discomfort. Each time we cope with fear without fleeing, we teach our mind and body that we are safer than we believed. Each time we question a negative thought, we loosen its hold on us. Over time, this steady process can reduce how much fear and anxiety control our life.

Recognizing Your Triggers in Daily Life

Paying attention to when fear or anxiety appears can help us notice common triggers. You might see that you often feel anxious right before going to bed, or when you have to make an important phone call, or after reading certain news stories.

Once you see the pattern, you can prepare. If bedtime sets off anxious thoughts, you can create a short wind-down routine to calm yourself. If phone calls spark fear, you can practice small scripts or reminders that you have done this before and survived. By planning for triggers, you do not wait until the last minute when the fear is strongest.

Replacing Old Reactions with New Steps

Imagine your typical reaction to a scary trigger is to avoid it or freeze up. Now picture trying a small new step. Instead of running away, you pause, breathe, and challenge the thought. You might still feel uneasy, but you do not let it grow out of control. This new step is a small victory.

Repetition of these small steps changes the mind over time. At first, it might feel strange or forced. You might think, "This won't work for me." But with practice, these new ways can become part of your normal response, slowly rewiring how you handle fear.

The Role of Hope

Hope is the sense that things can get better. It is important in this process because without hope, we might see no reason to try. Hope does not mean denying the real challenges we face. It means believing that we can take steps, however small, to improve our situation.

When we have hope, we are more willing to test new strategies. We are more open to the idea that we are not locked in fear forever. This does not mean we expect life to be perfect. It only means we believe we have the power to make changes.

Putting It All Together: A First Look

We have seen that thoughts fuel feelings, and feelings push us toward certain actions. When fear or anxiety grows, it often starts with a thought—even if it is very quick. That thought might say, "I cannot handle this," or "Something terrible is about to happen." Our body reacts by tensing up. We feel uneasy or scared. Then we might try to avoid or escape. This sets up a loop that can become a pattern in our lives.

But we are not helpless. By noticing and questioning the thoughts, we can change how we feel and what we do next. This is not simple or instant, but each step builds on the one before it. As we move through this book, we will explore more ways to break the loop and find calmer responses.

Conclusion of Chapter 3

Our thoughts can shape our world. When they lean toward fear or worry, our emotions and bodies follow, feeding anxiety. But when we notice and challenge these thoughts, we can lessen their grip. This does not remove every moment of fear from life, but it can help us feel more secure and steady.

CHAPTER 4: OUTSIDE FACTORS THAT FEED FEAR AND ANXIETY

Introduction

We have explored how thoughts and feelings shape our reactions. Now we look beyond our mind and body to the world around us. Outside factors can play a huge role in making fear and anxiety worse. These factors can include our work setting, social ties, family traditions, and even news or social media.

Many of us try to fight our worries without changing our surroundings. That can be like swimming against a strong current. If our daily environment pushes us toward stress and fear, we may struggle to find relief. By spotting the outside factors that affect us, we can make changes that reduce the tension.

The Role of Social Pressures

We live in a world where social acceptance seems to matter a lot. We often hear messages that we should be popular, successful, or always in control. These messages can seep into our minds and cause us to doubt ourselves if we do not meet the expected standards.

Social pressures may also come from friends or family who expect certain behavior. For instance, a parent might expect their child to always achieve top grades, leaving the child terrified of failure. A friend might pressure us to act a certain way to fit in with the group. These outside expectations can trigger fear of not being enough or fear of being judged.

Cultural Messages and Media Influence

News channels, online feeds, and social media can also spark fear or anxiety. Headlines often focus on dangerous or negative events. While being informed is important, a steady stream of scary news can make the world seem more threatening than it might be.

Social media can feed anxiety by showing us only the best moments from other people's lives, leading us to feel our own life is lacking. We might compare ourselves to edited pictures or success stories and think, "I am falling behind." This sense of comparison can lead to a hidden fear that we will never measure up.

Stressful Events and Ongoing Uncertainty

Big life changes, such as moving, job loss, or relationship problems, can create a sense of dread. Even smaller changes, like shifting routines or dealing with an unexpected bill, can pile up and cause tension. When we face many changes at once, our mind may see the world as unstable.

Ongoing uncertainty can keep anxiety high. If we never know what the next day will bring, our minds might stay on high alert, scanning for trouble. This is common in places where the economy is shaky or where personal safety is not guaranteed.

Workplace Demands

Many people spend a large part of their day at work. If the workplace is filled with stress, deadlines, or competition, it can feed anxiety. If a boss is overly critical or if coworkers create tension, fear might build up. We might worry about losing our position or missing a big deadline.

We might also fall into the trap of perfection, thinking we must never make a mistake at work. This puts constant pressure on us, leading to worry and sleepless nights. Over time, it can result in burnout, which only increases fear of failing.

Family Dynamics

Family ties can be a source of support, but they can also spark fear and worry. If a household is marked by conflict, secrets, or strict rules, anxiety might become a normal state. People might not feel safe expressing how they really feel, which builds tension inside.

Sometimes family members send messages that make us doubt ourselves. They might call us names, judge us harshly, or blame us for things outside our control. These messages can linger, shaping how we see the world. If we were raised in a fearful home, we might pick up an ongoing sense that life is dangerous.

Financial Pressures

Money problems can cause deep worry. Fear of not being able to pay bills or losing a home can feel overwhelming. Even if we have enough to get by, the worry that it might not last can create ongoing tension.

Financial stress can also make us feel shame if we think we should be more successful. We might compare ourselves to friends or coworkers and feel anxious about not keeping up. This can lead to risky financial choices or avoidance of the issue, which in turn makes the stress worse.

The Effect of Physical Surroundings

Physical surroundings can also feed anxiety. If we live in a place with high crime rates, we might feel unsafe going out. If our home is cluttered or in disrepair, we might feel a constant sense of chaos. Even factors like noise, lighting, or lack of personal space can weigh on us.

In crowded cities, some people feel anxious in packed trains or busy streets. They might worry about being crushed or not able to escape quickly. In quiet rural areas, others might feel anxious due to isolation or lack of nearby help. These surroundings can act as triggers, reminding us of threats or feeding a sense of unease.

Unhealthy Relationships

Our ties with others can either ease our worries or make them worse. If we have a partner or friend who puts us down, we might develop ongoing anxiety about making them angry or losing their approval. This can erode our self-confidence over time.

Unhealthy relationships can also be ones where we feel responsible for the other person's mood. If they blame us whenever something goes wrong, we may live on edge, always trying to keep the peace. This can lead to a belief that we must control everything or risk conflict.

Cultural Expectations and Stigma

In some cultures, speaking about fear or anxiety can be frowned upon. People might expect us to appear strong or calm at all times. As a result, we might hide our worries, which only makes them worse. We may not seek help because we fear being labeled weak or lazy.

Cultural stigma can also make us deny that we have any problem until it becomes too large to handle. By then, anxiety might have taken a firm hold. Recognizing these cultural influences can help us see that the problem is not just inside us, but also in the messages we receive from society.

Technology and Constant Connectivity

Being always connected can feed anxiety. If our phone is always buzzing with alerts or if we feel compelled to check messages, we never fully relax. We might worry we will miss important news or look rude if we do not respond right away.

Constant connectivity can also disturb our sleep. Scrolling through feeds late at night can keep our mind active when it needs to wind down. The bright screens and endless stream of information can make us more alert, which fuels fear if we stumble on alarming stories or posts.

The Challenge of Setting Boundaries

When outside factors build pressure on us, one solution is to set boundaries. But this can be hard. We might fear that people will not accept our limits or that we will lose relationships if we say "no." We might also worry about missing out on news or social events if we cut back on phone time.

Yet boundaries can be crucial to reduce stress. For instance, we might set a rule to stop reading news after a certain time in the evening, or to say no to extra tasks at work when we are already overloaded. We might also limit the time we spend with people who make us feel afraid or drained.

Creating a Supportive Environment

It can help to shape our environment in ways that bring calm. If clutter makes us anxious, we can take small steps to tidy up. If noise at home is a problem, we can use headphones with soothing sounds or find a quieter corner if possible.

We can also look for communities or groups that understand what we are going through. Talking with others who face similar fears can help us feel less alone. Even online forums, if used wisely, can provide some sense of belonging and support.

Why We Cannot Always Change Our Surroundings

Not everyone can control their outside world as much as they want. Maybe we cannot change jobs right now, or we cannot move away from a noisy or unsafe neighborhood. Maybe we have responsibilities that make it hard to set strict limits with certain people.

In these cases, we work with what we have. We learn to adapt our responses. We use the thought and feeling tools discussed in Chapter 3 to cope with triggers we cannot remove. We find small ways to reduce their impact, like taking brief breaks during a stressful day.

The Value of Healthy Activities

Outside factors do not have to be negative. We can choose some that reduce fear and anxiety. Activities like gentle exercise, time in nature, or listening to music can calm the mind. Spending time with kind people who show understanding can help us relax and feel safe.

We can look for small pockets of rest in our day. Even a few minutes of quiet can make a difference if we are in a chaotic environment. Doing something creative or engaging our hands in a simple task can also pull our focus away from worry.

Identifying the Sources of External Stress

A helpful exercise is to list the top outside stressors in our life. We might write:

- **Difficult boss**

- Constant noise outside home
- Family fights
- News overload

By naming them, we see them more clearly. Then we can brainstorm ways to lessen their impact. Maybe we can change the times we deal with them or plan breaks in between. If our boss is difficult, maybe we can schedule short meetings instead of long ones or request a different style of feedback.

The Social Side of Fear

Fear can spread in groups. If the people around us are always talking about dangers or telling scary stories, we might feel that fear is everywhere. Social media groups can sometimes amplify worries, passing on rumors or focusing on the worst events.

When we notice this, we can take a step to protect ourselves. We do not have to argue with others, but we can decide how much time we spend in these fearful discussions. We can also look for balanced views that provide facts instead of just rumors or gloom.

Standing Up for Your Needs

It takes courage to tell others we need space or a change of pace. We might worry that we will upset them or that they will see us as weak. But standing up for our needs is often a key part of cutting down fear. If we keep everything hidden, we allow outside stressors to keep piling on us.

Standing up for our needs can be a small step, like telling a friend, "I am feeling overwhelmed, so I need a quieter evening," or letting a family member know, "I need you to speak more calmly if we want to fix this issue." Even if it does not solve every problem, it can reduce some anxiety by giving us a sense of control.

Keeping Perspective on Outside Events

Many outside factors are beyond our control. The weather, world politics, or economic shifts can all add worry to our lives. We might fear a storm or a recession, wondering how it will affect us. While we cannot stop these events, we can work on keeping perspective.

Ask, "What can I do to prepare for this issue in a practical way?" If there is a storm warning, gather essentials or make a plan to stay safe. If there is news about economic trouble, see if you can save a small amount or look for community support. By focusing on steps we can take, we shift our mind from panic to action.

How Environment and Mindset Interact

Our environment can spark fear, but our mindset can magnify or reduce it. Two people in the same stressful setting might react in very different ways. One might spiral into anxiety, while the other finds small ways to cope and remain calm. This does not mean one is better than the other. It means their thought patterns and coping skills differ.

Over time, by changing our mindset, we might find that our surroundings bother us less. Or we might realize we can handle them in ways that once seemed impossible. When our thoughts shift, we gain more freedom to choose how to respond to external pressures.

Conclusion of Chapter 4

Outside factors play a large role in fueling **fear** and **anxiety**. These can include social pressures, family dynamics, news overload, workplace stress, and more. Recognizing them is vital because it helps us see that fear is not just an internal flaw. Often, our outside world adds to the problem.

By being aware of these forces, we can plan ways to lessen their impact or protect ourselves when we cannot remove them. We can set boundaries, find supportive communities, reduce our media intake, or speak up for our needs. We can also work on our mindset to keep a healthy balance between being informed and feeling overwhelmed.

Part Two of our book has focused on triggers and the first steps we can take. In Chapter 3, we explored how our thoughts and feelings shape our reactions and how questioning negative thoughts can reduce fear. In Chapter 4, we saw how outside pressures can feed or spark fear and anxiety and discovered that changing our environment can sometimes help.

PART THREE: SKILLS FOR DAILY LIFE

You have learned about the nature of **fear** and **anxiety**, as well as the triggers that can spark them. Now we will turn to ways you can reduce that inner storm and find more calm in day-to-day living. **Part Three** focuses on **skills for daily life**. In Chapter 5, we will look at methods to calm tension and stress whenever they appear. In Chapter 6, we will see how building steady routines can create an inner sense of peace.

Each idea may speak to you in a different way, so do not worry if one strategy feels more useful than another. The goal is to gather a set of tools that you can use in different moments. Over time, you can mix and match these ideas in a way that suits your own style and needs.

CHAPTER 5: WAYS TO CALM TENSION AND STRESS

Introduction

Daily life can pile on stress in many forms. We might rush from one place to another, handle tough people at work or home, and still find ourselves overloaded with tasks. This load of stress can fuel our **fear** and **anxiety**, leaving us on edge.

Yet there are small, steady ways to let go of tension. Some involve our body, like simple breath routines or gentle movements. Others target our mind, such as letting go of worries by focusing on something else for a moment. These methods may not solve every big problem, but they can give us a break and stop fear from building too high.

In this chapter, we will explore a range of helpful practices. Each is easy to learn. You can do some of them quietly at home, and others you can do wherever you are. The idea is to handle stress at an early stage before it turns into overwhelming panic.

The Value of Slow Breathing

One of the quickest ways to calm tension is through **slow breathing**. When we feel anxious or scared, our breath often becomes fast and shallow. This signals our body that something is wrong. By making our breaths slower and deeper, we send a message that we are safe.

A simple method is to inhale slowly for a count of four, hold the breath for a brief moment, and exhale slowly for a count of four. If you are in a hurry, even one or two slow breaths can help. Doing this at regular points in the day can create a rhythm that lowers stress.

Try placing a hand on your lower belly. Feel it rise with each breath in and fall with each breath out. This helps direct the air deeper into your lungs, easing tension in your chest and shoulders. Over time, slow breathing can become a natural response when fear or worry shows up.

Progressive Muscle Relaxation

Another way to reduce tension is by using **progressive muscle relaxation**. This involves tensing and then releasing different groups of muscles in your body. You can start at your feet and work your way up, or begin at your head and move down.

For example, focus on your toes. Curl them tight for a slow count of five, then let them relax completely. Notice the difference between tension and relaxation. Then move to your calves. Tighten them for five counts, then let go. Continue this all the way up your body—thighs, stomach, back, shoulders, arms, hands, and so on.

This exercise helps you see how it feels when muscles are tense and how it feels when they are relaxed. Many of us hold tension without noticing it. By doing this exercise, we train our body to let go of that tightness. This often eases anxious thoughts, too, because our mind and body are linked.

The Use of Grounding Techniques

Grounding is a term for methods that bring our focus back to the present moment. When we are in fear or anxiety, our thoughts often jump to the past or future. We worry about what might go wrong, or we recall something that made us scared before. Grounding brings our attention back to what is happening right here, right now.

One grounding method is the **Five Senses** approach. It goes like this:

- Look around and name **five** things you can see.
- Name **four** things you can feel with your sense of touch.
- Name **three** things you can hear.
- Name **two** things you can smell.
- Name **one** thing you can taste or something that reminds you of taste.

This might seem simple, but it works well. It reminds our mind that in this moment, we are present, and many threats we imagine might not be happening right now. This can slow the rush of panic and bring us back to a calmer state.

Another grounding trick is to pick something in your immediate area and describe it in great detail to yourself. Maybe it is a mug on your table. Notice the color, the shape, the texture. By doing this, you train your mind to focus on the real world, not on fears and worries.

Self-Soothing Methods

Self-soothing means treating yourself with kindness when stress flares up. This can include something as small as placing a hand on your chest and noticing the warmth. The goal is to provide a gentle sense of comfort that helps calm fear.

Some people find that **positive self-talk** works well here. They might say in their mind, "I am allowed to feel worried, but I am also safe right now." Another example is, "I am doing my best, and that is enough." These statements do not have to be fancy. They just need to be honest and reassuring.

Others use small physical items to feel safer. They might hold a smooth stone or wear a piece of jewelry that has a calming meaning. These items can remind them of calm moments or supportive thoughts.

Shifting Attention from Worry

Worry often grows when we focus on the same thought again and again. An effective way to reduce its power is by shifting our attention for a bit. This does not mean we are ignoring real problems, but rather giving our mind a break so it does not spiral.

Some easy ways to shift attention include:

- Doing a simple chore like washing dishes and focusing on the water and the soap bubbles.
- Listening to a favorite song and paying attention to each instrument.
- Working on a puzzle or coloring.
- Taking a short walk and noticing the air on your skin or the details of the path.

These small acts give our mind a pause. Afterward, we can return to the problem with a clearer head. Sometimes, stepping away from the cycle of worry opens up new ideas on how to handle the issue.

Simple Mindfulness Practice

Mindfulness is about paying attention to the present moment without harsh judgment. You can practice it in daily life by focusing on one thing at a time. For instance, if you are eating a snack, notice its taste, texture, smell, and how it feels when you chew.

When anxious thoughts pop up, you do not force them away. Instead, you note them: "I notice I am thinking about tomorrow's meeting." Then you gently bring your attention back to the snack in front of you. This can be done with any activity—walking, showering, reading, or talking with someone.

By training ourselves to stay in the present, we weaken the habit of worrying about what happened before or what might happen later. Over time, mindfulness can reduce the background noise of fear. It does not remove every concern, but it lowers our tendency to leap into worst-case ideas.

The Power of Gentle Movement

Physical movement can help burn off the excess energy that fear and anxiety stir up in our bodies. This does not need to be a tough workout. Even gentle movement like slow stretches, basic yoga poses, or a short walk can help.

When we move, our body releases certain chemicals that can lift our mood. Our muscles also get a chance to release tension, and our breath often settles into a calmer pattern. If you like to walk, try a few minutes of walk every day. If you enjoy stretching, set aside a small space to stretch your body in the morning or evening.

Some people combine gentle movement with music or calming sounds. That adds another layer of relaxation. The key is not to force yourself through an intense session you hate, but to find small ways to move that feel okay and safe to you.

Journaling for Clarity

Writing in a journal can help us process stress and fear. By putting words on paper, we give ourselves a way to see what is going on in our mind. We can spot patterns or hidden worries. Sometimes, the act of writing itself releases tension.

You can write about anything that concerns you. There is no perfect format. Some people jot down their daily thoughts, while others write letters they never send, or lists of things that bother them. The main point is to allow the mind to express worries so they do not stay locked inside.

If you find it helpful, you can close each journal entry with a short note of **gratitude**: something in your life that is going okay or a small moment of peace you had that day. This does not mean you deny problems. It is just a way to remind yourself there can be bits of light even when fear is present.

Using Music and Sounds to Calm

Music can have a direct impact on our mood. Some songs energize us, while others help us relax. If you are feeling tense, try playing calm tracks at a soft volume. Or find nature sounds, like rain or gentle waves, and listen to them while sitting quietly.

Pay attention to how your body feels as you hear the music. Does your heartbeat slow a bit? Do your shoulders loosen? By noticing these changes, you reinforce the link between these sounds and a calmer state of mind. Over time, just starting your calming playlist might trigger your body to relax.

Art as a Stress Outlet

Creating something can help release the pressure of fear. It could be drawing, painting, knitting, or any other form of art. Even if you think you are not good at it, the act of creation can shift your focus away from worry.

When you are making art, your mind often goes into a gentle flow. You might lose track of time. This break from fearful thoughts can be refreshing. Later, you might feel a bit lighter, with more room in your head for clear thinking.

Talking It Out with a Supportive Friend

Sometimes, the best relief for tension is to share our thoughts with someone we trust. Fear can grow large in our heads when we are alone with it. Talking it out can help us realize we are not alone, and it can offer new viewpoints.

We do not have to talk to someone who has all the answers. Even a friend who simply listens can be a huge help. Speaking our worries aloud can bring clarity. We might hear ourselves and think, "Actually, this problem might not be as big as I thought."

Having a Safe Space at Home

If possible, create a small area in your home that feels calm. It might be a corner of your room with a soft cushion, a blanket, or a small lamp. When fear or anxiety spike, you can go to this spot for a few minutes.

In that safe space, you might keep a journal, headphones for music, or items that help you feel secure. The idea is to build a physical reminder that you can step out of the chaos around you and recenter yourself. Over time, sitting in this spot might become a signal to your mind that it is time to unwind.

Gradual Exposure to Uncomfortable Situations

Sometimes, tension and stress come from avoiding things that scare us. The more we avoid them, the bigger they seem in our minds. A long-term way to reduce fear is through **gradual exposure**—facing the scary thing in small steps that feel manageable.

For instance, if speaking in front of others is terrifying, you might start by talking in front of a mirror. Then you might practice with a friend. Later, you might speak to a small group you trust before moving to bigger settings.

Each step helps your mind and body learn that you can handle a bit more fear than you thought. Over time, this can lower the overall tension you feel in those moments. While this is not an instant fix, it is a powerful way to keep fear from running your life.

Setting Small Goals for Each Day

Sometimes, our fear about the future makes us forget what we can do right now. Setting small goals each day can help ground us. Maybe your goal is to take one short walk, or write for ten minutes, or spend a few minutes doing slow breathing.

These goals do not have to be big. The key is that they are clear and doable. When you meet them, you remind yourself that you can follow through on something. This boosts confidence. It also reduces the aimless worry that can build when we feel we are not making any progress.

Reducing Self-Criticism

Many people who struggle with fear or anxiety also tend to be hard on themselves. They might call themselves lazy for feeling scared, or weak for not being able to just "get over it." This self-criticism only adds more stress.

Try to replace self-criticism with gentle honesty. You can say, "I feel anxious, and that is okay. I am doing something about it by using my skills." This does not ignore that you have fear; it just refuses to make it worse by attacking yourself.

If you find this tough, think of how you would talk to a friend who feels scared. You would probably be understanding and kind. That same tone can work wonders for your own stress levels.

Rest and Sleep as Key Factors

A tired mind is more prone to fear. When we lack sleep, our body's stress response can be overactive. We might also find it harder to think clearly or handle daily ups and downs. This is why **rest** is not a luxury; it is essential.

Try to build a bedtime habit that helps you relax. Lower bright lights, keep screens away for at least half an hour before sleep, and do something gentle like reading a calm book or listening to soft music. If worrisome thoughts appear at night, keep a notepad by your bed. Write them down and remind yourself you will revisit them the next day.

Why Consistency Matters

Many of these methods work best when used often, not just in emergencies. Think of them like building blocks for a calmer mind. Each time you practice slow breathing or a grounding technique, you strengthen your ability to handle the next wave of fear.

We might not see the change all at once. But over weeks or months, consistent use of these skills can make a noticeable difference. We might find ourselves bouncing back from a scare faster, or we might sleep better because our stress levels are lower.

Handling Stress at Work or School

In busy places like work or school, we may have limited time to manage fear. Still, we can use micro-breaks. If you have 30 seconds, you can do one slow breath and relax your shoulders. If you have two minutes, you can step out for a quick walk or find a quiet corner to regroup.

You can also plan a short break during lunch or between tasks to stretch or do a grounding exercise. Letting yourself rest, even for a few moments, can stop stress from piling too high. Over time, these small breaks can keep you from getting stuck in a constant state of anxiety.

Using Humor to Break Tension

Humor can help reduce the hold of fear. Watching a funny video, remembering a silly moment, or sharing a light joke with a friend can shift your mindset. Laughter triggers the release of certain chemicals that lower stress and help us relax.

This does not mean laughing at your fear or ignoring it. It means giving yourself permission to have a light moment, even when things are tough. That pause can break the tension, allowing you to return to your tasks with a fresher mind.

A Simple Plan for Tense Days

When you wake up feeling worried or tense, it might help to make a plan for small self-care actions. Maybe you decide to do a three-minute slow breathing break every couple of hours. Or you aim to step outside for fresh air in the afternoon. Having a simple plan can guide you when fear flares up.

If unexpected stress appears, you can refer back to your plan: "What was that quick thing I said I would do to calm down?" By sticking to the plan, you lessen the chance of being swept away by panic.

Checking for Balance in Activity

Sometimes, fear can push us into extremes. We might overwork to avoid scary thoughts, or we might avoid all tasks because we feel overwhelmed. Both extremes feed stress. A healthy balance means giving some time to tasks, some time to rest, and some time to play or do relaxing hobbies.

You can do a quick check at the end of the day: "Did I spend all day working without any break? Did I spend the day avoiding what I need to do?" Adjusting little by little can help you find a more balanced rhythm, reducing the triggers for anxiety.

The Place of Professional Help

Calming methods are helpful, but if fear or anxiety feel too big to manage, you might consider seeking professional help. This could mean talking with a counselor, therapist, or other mental health professional. They can offer tailored strategies for your situation.

There is no shame in reaching out for that help. Sometimes we need extra support or a fresh perspective. Professionals can also introduce you to guided methods that go deeper than the basics we are discussing.

Conclusion of Chapter 5

In this chapter, you explored many ways to calm tension and stress. These range from slow breathing and muscle relaxation to grounding techniques, gentle movement, and more. Each method can help you keep fear from running wild. Over time, using these skills on a regular basis can make a big difference in how you cope with daily challenges.

As you try these tools, remember that small steps matter. You do not have to tackle everything at once. If one approach does not feel right, try another. The key is to build a personal set of calming skills that you can call on when fear or anxiety begin to rise.

Next, we will look at **Chapter 6**, where we explore how to **use steady routines** to support a calmer mind. While the methods in this chapter focus on in-the-moment relief, routines aim to prevent stress from piling up in the first place. Both are important parts of creating a balanced daily life.

CHAPTER 6: USING STEADY ROUTINES FOR INNER PEACE

Introduction

We often think fear and anxiety strike out of nowhere, but they can build over time when our daily habits leave us worn down or uneasy. One of the best ways to keep anxiety at a more manageable level is by having **steady routines**. These routines can provide comfort, reduce uncertainty, and help us feel more in control.

In this chapter, we will discuss how routines help the mind, how to create them, and how they can guard us against stress. We will also look at ways to keep routines flexible so that they do not become a source of pressure.

The Protective Power of Routines

Routines act like anchors in our daily life. They give our mind and body signals about what is coming next, which can reduce the unknown. When we know we will wake up, do a short stretch, have a simple breakfast, and then head to our tasks, it removes some of the guesswork.

This matters because the unknown is often a big trigger for fear. If every day feels chaotic, our mind stays alert, scanning for threats. With a routine, we build a sense of order. Even if other parts of life remain uncertain, these small regular actions can provide a stable base.

Morning Routines to Set the Tone

How we start our day can influence our mood for hours. If we jump out of bed at the last minute and rush around, we may feel stressed before the day truly begins. A morning routine does not have to be long. Even ten or fifteen minutes of calm can help.

One idea is to do a brief **stretch** while focusing on your breath. You might then sip a warm drink in a quiet space. If you pray or have a simple reading you like, you can do that, too. Some people enjoy writing a few lines in a journal about what they hope to do that day.

The point is to avoid flipping immediately into worry mode. By setting a calm tone in the morning, we give ourselves a bit more space to handle any stress that appears later.

Evening Routines for Better Rest

When we end the day, a routine can help us let go of the noise in our head. Without it, we might slide into bed with our mind still racing about the day's events or tomorrow's worries. That can lead to shallow sleep or nightmares, which then fuel more anxiety.

A helpful evening routine might include **turning off screens** or setting them aside at least half an hour before bedtime. We can use soft lighting and do something gentle like reading, light stretching, or listening to calm music. If thoughts keep popping up, we can jot them down in a "worry journal" to deal with the next day.

By repeating a soothing evening ritual, we teach our body that it is time to wind down. Over time, this can improve the quality of our rest, making us more resilient to fear.

Meal Times as Points of Stability

We might think of meals as just times to eat, but they can also provide structure. Eating at regular times, if our schedule allows, can prevent the stress that comes from hunger or low energy. Skipping meals or eating at odd hours might make the mind more prone to anxious thoughts.

We can also use mealtime as a mindful break. Instead of rushing, we could try to slow down a bit—taste our food, notice the textures, and pause between bites. This helps our body relax and also prevents mindless snacking or over-eating in response to stress.

Work and Study Routines

Whether we work at an office, at home, or attend classes, having set periods for tasks can reduce worry. If we know that from 9 to 10 we will focus on a key project, then from 10 to 10:15 we take a short break, our mind can settle into that pattern.

Breaks are important, too. Working non-stop can lead to burnout, which raises anxiety. Scheduling short rests every couple of hours can help us reset our mind. During these breaks, we can practice any calming skill from Chapter 5, like slow breathing or a quick walk.

Balancing Activity and Rest

Routines are not just about doing tasks; they also include rest. Many people feel anxious because they never switch off their "work mode." If we plan time for relaxation, we remove some of that guilt or feeling that we should always be busy.

For instance, you might decide that after dinner, you will spend 30 minutes on a relaxing activity like reading, gentle exercise, or even a calm show if it helps you unwind. This is not wasted time. It is a necessary part of caring for your mind and body.

Setting Goals for Routine Building

When we try to create new routines, it helps to set clear goals. For example, you might decide:

- "I will wake up 15 minutes earlier to have a calm cup of tea before I start my day."
- "I will switch off my phone at 9 PM to reduce my screen time before bed."
- "I will take a 5-minute walk at lunch each day."

These small, specific goals make it easier to track your progress. You can also adjust them if you find they do not fit your life. The key is consistency. Even if we miss a day, we can come back the next day and start again.

Why Flexibility Matters

Routines bring order, but being too rigid can cause stress when unexpected events happen. Suppose your routine is to read in the evening, but a friend calls needing help. If you become upset because your routine is interrupted, that can spark more anxiety.

Being flexible means allowing changes when real life gets in the way. We can adapt by maybe reading for just five minutes later or finding another moment to relax. The point of routines is to lower stress, not to add more. So we hold them as guides rather than strict laws.

Habit Stacking to Build Routines

A helpful technique is called "habit stacking," where you link a new habit to something you already do. For example:

- If you want to do slow breathing each morning, tie it to making coffee. While the coffee is brewing, you stand there and do one minute of breath work.
- If you want to stretch each evening, do it right after brushing your teeth.

By attaching the new habit to an old one, you are more likely to remember it and make it stick. Over time, these small routines can blend seamlessly into your day.

Handling Setbacks in Routine

No one's routine is perfect all the time. We might travel, face an emergency, or simply have an off day. During such times, it is easy to feel we failed. But it is better to see it as a pause rather than a failure.

When life calms down again, we step back into our routine. If the break lasted a long time, we might need to rebuild slowly. That is okay. The important thing is to keep the idea of routine as a support tool, not as something that makes us feel guilty.

The Mental Benefits of Routine

Routines do more than structure our day. They also reduce decision fatigue. When we know what to do next, we spend less energy worrying or planning. This frees mental space for creative thinking or problem-solving.

They also give a sense of achievement. When we stick to a routine, even if it is small, we can say, "I did what I set out to do today." This builds our confidence and can push away the fear that we are not in control.

Social Routines and Support

We can also build routines with other people. For instance, having a certain night each week for a friend chat or family gathering. This can strengthen our support network, which in turn helps reduce fear.

If we often feel lonely or anxious, a social routine can give us something to look forward to. It also helps us stay connected, so we have people to lean on when anxiety flares up.

Outdoor Time and Routines

Spending time outdoors can be a key part of a calming routine. Fresh air, sunlight, or a view of trees and sky can lower stress. If you live in a city, you might find a nearby park or a quiet street to walk once a day.

Try to make it a set time, maybe in the morning or after work. When this becomes a habit, your body and mind start to expect that daily pause. Nature has a calming effect on many people, so even a short trip outside can help.

Screen Management

Many of us spend a lot of time on our phones, computers, or watching TV. While technology can be useful, it can also feed anxiety if we do not set limits. Scrolling through bad news late at night can make it hard to sleep.

A routine around screen time can help. For instance, no phones at the dinner table, or no screens after a certain hour in the evening. Setting these rules for yourself (and sharing them with family or friends if you live together) can reduce stress. It also helps free up time for more restful activities.

Personalizing Your Routine

What calms one person might not calm another. Some people feel better after a brisk walk; others need something quieter like reading or meditating. The key is to try different activities and see what fits your life and preferences.

You might write a short list of activities that leave you feeling peaceful. Then see where they fit in your day. If mornings are hectic, a short breathing break might be all you can do. If evenings are free, maybe that is the time for a more involved routine like a hot bath or some creative work.

Tracking Progress Gently

Some people find it helpful to keep a simple log of their daily habits. It might be a planner where you check off each routine as you do it. Or you could use a small app that reminds you of your goals.

Tracking helps you see patterns. You might notice that on days you do your morning routine, your overall anxiety is lower. That can motivate you to continue. Just be sure not to turn the tracking into a source of stress. If you miss a day, you note it and move on.

Combining Routines with In-the-Moment Calming

Routines help prevent fear from growing too large, but we still need quick methods like the ones in Chapter 5 for sudden stress. The best approach often blends the two: steady, daily habits that keep our baseline calm, and quick responses for surprise moments of anxiety.

For example, you might do a consistent morning routine, a stable work routine, and a calming evening routine. Then, if panic strikes in the middle of the day, you use a grounding technique. This layered approach can give you the strongest defense against fear.

The Long-Term Effects of Steady Routines

Over time, routines can help your mind trust that you are safe and capable of handling daily events. Each day you follow a basic structure, you reinforce the idea that life has order. Even if big problems appear, you have a base of healthy habits to steady you.

Many people find that after months of sticking to routines, they have fewer spikes of anxious worry. They might still feel stress in certain situations, but their overall coping ability is stronger. This does not mean life is without challenges. It just means we have a sturdier foundation to face those challenges.

When Routines Become Too Strict

While routines are helpful, there is a risk of becoming too attached to them. If we feel we must follow them exactly or else we panic, then the routine itself becomes a source of anxiety. This can happen if we see routines as rules that cannot bend.

To avoid this, remember to keep a bit of flexibility. Sometimes, life will shift your schedule. Instead of feeling everything is ruined, adjust for the day and move on. The routine is there to serve you, not the other way around.

Building Routines with Others

If you live with family or roommates, it can help to include them in parts of your routine. Maybe you all plan a shared dinner time or a short walk together in the evening. Working as a team can make the routines stronger, and it also builds a sense of community.

That said, it is okay if not everyone wants to join. You can still have personal routines that help you feel calm and balanced. Each person might have their own style, and that is fine.

Adapting to Life Changes

Life never stays the same. You might change jobs, move to a new place, or have shifts in your family life. When these changes happen, routines might need an update. For example, if you move to a different neighborhood, your old walking path might not be there. You can find a new path or another activity that fills the same role.

This process is normal. Instead of seeing it as an end to your progress, view it as an opportunity to refresh your routines. You might discover new ideas that help you even more than the old ones did.

The Confidence That Routines Bring

One reason routines help with fear is that they remind us we have control over some parts of life. Fear often grows when we feel helpless. By setting and following routines, we show ourselves that we can shape our day in positive ways.

This sense of control does not mean we can stop every bad thing from happening. But it does mean we have the power to create pockets of calm and order. That alone can reduce anxiety, because we know we can rely on certain parts of our day to ground us.

Blending Routines into a Bigger Plan

Along with the calming skills from Chapter 5, the routines we build in Chapter 6 form a strong base. Think of these two chapters as partners: one helps you with in-the-moment relief, and the other helps you prevent stress from rising too high in the first place.

As we continue in this book, we will look at more ways to work with your mind and break patterns that keep fear and anxiety locked in place. But remember that without daily habits, our progress can feel shaky. Routines give us a stable frame to build on.

Conclusion of Chapter 6

In this chapter, we have explored how steady routines offer a protective layer against **fear** and **anxiety**. By creating simple structures for our mornings, evenings, meals, and work breaks, we reduce the unknown and keep our minds calmer.

Routines do not have to be rigid. The best ones are flexible enough to handle life's changes. The idea is to have reliable anchors that bring a sense of peace and predictability. Over time, these routines become part of who we are, reminding us that we can face daily life with greater ease.

Part Three has now shown you key **skills for daily life**—calming methods and steady routines. As we move forward into **Part Four**, we will shift our focus to the mind itself. We will talk about specific techniques that help shape our thinking in a way that supports calm and self-confidence. The tools from Chapters 5 and 6 will blend with the mental exercises in the next chapters, giving us a well-rounded path to handle fear and anxiety in all parts of our lives.

PART FOUR: WORKING WITH THE MIND

You have explored many areas of **fear** and **anxiety** so far. Part One gave you an overview of these feelings. Part Two looked at triggers and first steps, and Part Three offered daily skills and routines to keep stress from piling up. Now, in **Part Four**, we will look deeper into the mind. We will learn specific approaches to guide your thoughts, strengthen your inner voice, and reduce the grip of negative beliefs. This part includes two chapters:

- Chapter 7: Techniques for a More Peaceful Mind
- Chapter 8: Building Inner Strength

Together, these chapters will help you see that how you think about events can change your emotional state in big ways. You will discover tools that reshape old thought patterns. You will also see how to spot the hidden beliefs that might be feeding your fear and anxiety. By the end of these chapters, you should have a clearer sense of how to work with your mind every day so that it supports a calmer life.

CHAPTER 7: TECHNIQUES FOR A MORE PEACEFUL MIND

Introduction

Our minds are powerful. They can paint bright images of what is possible, or they can trap us in circles of **worry** and fear. When we do not know how to guide our thoughts, we might feel pushed around by them. We may find ourselves stuck in doubt or replaying past mistakes. That can build up anxiety over time.

The good news is that the mind can learn new habits. Just as a musician learns to move their fingers across the keys, we can learn mental habits that lead to more peace. This chapter offers methods to help us calm mental chatter, question unhelpful ideas, and connect with a more balanced view of ourselves.

We will look at core concepts like **automatic thoughts**, **cognitive distortions**, and **reframing**. We will also explore how to work gently with these mental processes so we do not fall into the trap of trying to force our minds to be quiet. The aim is to guide your mind toward calm, not to fight it.

The Nature of Automatic Thoughts

Most of the thoughts we have each day arise without our conscious choice. We see someone frowning, and a thought appears that maybe they are upset with us. We notice our phone battery is low, and a thought pops up that we might miss an important call. These are called **automatic thoughts**.

Automatic thoughts can be helpful at times. They might alert us to real problems or guide us to do the right thing. However, when fear or anxiety shape these thoughts, they can become negative. They may jump to the worst outcome. They may flood us with doubt.

An example might be when someone is late to meet you, and you immediately think, "They do not respect me," or "I must have done something wrong," or "What if they had a car accident?" These are automatic thoughts that come so fast we do not always question them. We take them as truth.

By learning to spot these thoughts in the moment, we begin to take a step back from them. We can then check whether they match reality or if they are fueled by fear.

Recognizing Cognitive Distortions

Cognitive distortions are common patterns of thinking that twist how we see the world. They often feed fear and anxiety. By noticing these distortions, we can interrupt them before they build up too much stress. Here are some of the most common ones (written in simple terms to avoid fancy language):

1. **All-or-Nothing Thinking**: Seeing things as fully good or fully bad, with no middle ground.

2. **Overgeneralizing**: Drawing a broad conclusion from one event (for instance, failing once and deciding you always fail).
3. **Catastrophizing**: Imagining the worst possible outcome.
4. **Mind Reading**: Believing you know what others think about you, often assuming it is negative.
5. **Fortune Telling**: Predicting the future in a negative way without real proof.
6. **Discounting Positives**: Brushing off good things that happen or good qualities you have.

When you notice a wave of anxiety, see if you can spot any of these distortions. You might say, "I am catastrophizing right now," or "I am thinking in all-or-nothing terms." This label alone can help you step out of the spiral. Once you spot the distortion, you can check the facts more calmly.

Thought Records and Reality Checks

A powerful tool for changing negative thought patterns is the **thought record**. This involves writing down a situation, the automatic thoughts it sparked, how those thoughts made you feel, and what the facts really might be.

For instance, suppose you had a meeting with your boss, and afterward, you felt anxious. You write:

- **Situation**: Meeting with my boss.
- **Automatic Thought**: My boss thinks I am incompetent.
- **Feelings**: Anxiety, dread.
- **Check the Facts**: Did my boss say anything that indicated displeasure? Did they criticize my work? Often, we find no real proof.

Then you can write a **balanced thought**: "I do not know what my boss thinks of me. All I know is they asked for a review of the project. That is normal. They did not say I was failing."

Doing this kind of exercise trains you to look for evidence instead of blindly trusting every anxious thought. Over time, you might see a pattern in your negative thinking and learn to question it sooner.

The Power of Reframing

Reframing means taking a thought or situation and looking at it in a more helpful way. It is not about lying to yourself or pretending everything is fine. It is about shifting your viewpoint so you can see the full picture, not just the fearful part.

An example might be:

- **Negative Thought**: "I messed up my speech at work; I am such a failure."
- **Reframed Thought**: "I made some mistakes during my speech, but I finished it. There is a lot I can learn to do better next time."

This reframe does not pretend the mistake did not happen. It simply adds perspective. Mistakes can be chances to learn. By seeing them that way, we reduce the toxic shame that often comes with fear-based thinking.

Acceptance of Thoughts Instead of Fighting Them

One of the traps in working with the mind is the urge to make negative thoughts go away by sheer force. The problem is that resistance can increase stress. When we push down a thought, we might give it more power.

Acceptance here means letting the thought be present for a moment without believing it fully. You might say, "I notice I am thinking I will fail. It is just a thought. It does not have to define me or my future."

This approach comes from ideas often used in mindfulness-based methods. By allowing the thought to exist, you reduce the panic that grows when you see it as a monster you must destroy. When the urgency fades, you can calmly decide what to do next.

Self-Compassion in Dealing with the Mind

Fear and anxiety can be rough on how we treat ourselves. When we make a mistake, we might launch into harsh self-talk, calling ourselves weak or pathetic. This only piles more stress on top of the fear.

A more compassionate stance is to treat yourself as a close friend. You might say, "I feel worried, and that is understandable. Lots of people feel this way sometimes. It does not mean I am broken."

Self-compassion does not mean we ignore problems. It means we face them with kindness, which usually leads to a calmer mind that can focus on finding real solutions.

Visualization for Calming the Mind

Sometimes it helps to use simple visualization to guide the mind toward calm. This can be done by finding a quiet spot and imagining a peaceful scene. You could picture yourself sitting by a quiet lake or a cozy fireplace.

While you imagine this scene, pay attention to details. What does the air feel like? How does the water move? What is the temperature? The more details you include, the easier it is to shift from worry to a place of quiet in your mind.

Some people find it helpful to imagine breathing in calm air (or a soothing color) and breathing out tension (or a dark color). This is not magic; it is a mental tool that redirects your attention from fear to peace.

Graded Exposure in the Mind

In an earlier chapter, we mentioned taking small steps to face things that scare us. That is called gradual exposure. You can also do this in your mind, which is sometimes called "imaginal exposure."

First, you pick a situation that triggers fear, but you visualize it in small steps. If you fear flying, you might imagine sitting in the airport, noticing your feelings. Then you imagine stepping onto the plane, noticing the seat and the cabin. You picture the engine sound, the feeling of takeoff. You pause at each step to use calming methods.

This mental practice can help you get used to the feeling of facing the scary situation without actually being there yet. Over time, the mind can learn that while discomfort arises, you can still handle it.

Detachment from Negative Stories

Fear and anxiety can spin stories about who we are or what the future holds. We might say, "I am always unlucky," or "Things never work out for me." These are not just single thoughts; they are stories we tell ourselves.

Detachment means seeing these stories as narratives, not as fixed facts. We can notice them and say, "There goes that story about me being unlucky." This small shift creates distance. If it is just a story, we can choose not to put so much trust in it.

To practice this, try writing down the main "stories" that your anxiety tends to tell. Then, label them as stories. If you often think, "I am not capable," label it as "The Not Capable Story." The next time it appears, recognize it: "Oh, the Not Capable Story is showing up." This helps you remember it is one possible angle, not the ultimate truth.

Self-Talk Scripts for Anxiety

When anxiety spikes, it can help to have a small set of phrases ready. This is different from trying to block out thoughts. It is more like having a steady voice you can turn to in a storm.

Examples of such scripts might be:

- "I can be nervous and still move forward."
- "These are just feelings; they will pass."
- "I have felt this way before, and I got through it."

You can pick whatever words feel honest and calming to you. The idea is to speak to yourself in a clear, supportive tone, much like a coach would do in a tense moment.

The Role of Repetition in Changing Thoughts

Changing how we think is not a one-time event. Our minds have patterns set up over years. To shift them, we need repetition. Each time we catch a negative thought and question it, we weaken the old pattern. Each time we try a healthier thought or a calming script, we strengthen a new pattern.

It is similar to learning a new skill. Early on, we might slip back into old ways. We might forget to question our distortions or fail to spot an all-or-nothing thought. That is normal. Over time, the more we practice, the more natural it becomes to respond in a calmer way.

Consistency vs. Perfection

When working with the mind, people sometimes believe they must never have a negative thought again. That is unrealistic. The mind will always produce some worries, especially in stressful times.

The goal is not perfect control of every thought. The goal is a consistent effort to guide the mind back to balance when fear flares up. We want to reduce how often negative thoughts turn into full-blown panic. We want to shorten the time we spend in worry.

This consistent approach is much kinder than striving for an impossible standard. We accept that fear might appear, but we also trust in our ability to cope with it.

Using Mental Reminders in Daily Life

It helps to have short reminders scattered through your day. These can be physical notes or just something you say in your head. A reminder might be: "Check your thoughts," or "Is this thought based on facts?"

Some people use simple wristbands or phone alarms to prompt a quick mental check. When the phone chimes, they pause for a few seconds, notice any tension or negative thinking, and do a short calming breath. Such small breaks, repeated often, can weaken the cycle of worry.

Dealing with "What-If" Thinking

Many anxious thoughts start with "What if…" and then spin a negative scenario. We might say, "What if I lose my job?" or "What if my friend hates me now?" The mind can run wild with these questions, creating more stress.

One trick is to finish the question with, "What if that happens, and I find a way to handle it?" Instead of just picturing doom, include a realistic plan for coping. This does not guarantee the outcome you want, but it reminds you that you have options.

Another approach is to limit "what-if" thinking to a set time. Tell yourself you will spend ten minutes a day exploring these worries. When they show up outside that time, gently remind yourself that you have a worry appointment later, and return your focus to the present moment.

Mental Flexibility: Letting Go of Rigid Ideas

Fear can make us cling to rigid beliefs, like "I must always be liked," or "I must never fail." When life challenges those beliefs, we feel intense anxiety.

Mental flexibility is the skill of allowing more nuanced beliefs. We might say, "I want to be liked, but not everyone will like me. That is normal." Or, "I do not want to fail, but mistakes can happen, and I can learn from them."

This kind of flexible thinking reduces the tension that arises when real life does not match our rigid rules. It does not mean we stop caring; it means we accept that we cannot control every outcome.

Labeling the Mind's Activity

Sometimes we get lost in a storm of thoughts and do not even realize it. A technique to help with this is labeling. When you notice your mind chasing a worry, you can say, "Thinking." When you notice your mind flipping to a memory, say, "Remembering." If it starts judging, say, "Judging."

This label interrupts the mental flow for a moment, letting you see what is happening. Once you label it, you can choose to refocus on your present task, or you can try a calming approach. This does not solve every worry, but it can prevent you from slipping too far into old spirals.

Facing the Unknown with Curiosity

Fear often arises from the unknown. We think, "I do not know how this will turn out," and our mind fills that gap with scary outcomes. One way to work with this is to adopt a bit of curiosity: "I do not know how this will turn out, and that is part of life. Let me see what happens."

This stance can take practice, because fear craves certainty. But life rarely gives us total certainty. When we replace the demand to know everything with a willingness to learn from whatever comes, we reduce some of the panic that arises from not knowing.

Turning Mistakes into Data

Fear tells us that mistakes define us or mark us as flawed. A different angle is to see mistakes as data. When something goes wrong, we can look at what happened, figure out why, and adjust next time.

This mindset is often used in science. Experiments fail, but each failure provides data that leads to new attempts. If we bring that mindset to our daily life, each slip or error can become a chance to refine our approach, rather than a sign we are doomed.

The Balance of Logic and Emotion

Some people try to handle fear by only using logic, ignoring their emotions. Others believe they must always follow their emotions and ignore facts. Both extremes can cause problems. A more balanced method is to listen to emotions but still check them against facts.

For example, if you feel anxious about a test, your emotion might say, "I am not ready." You can check the facts: "I studied every day this week, and I did well on practice questions." You do not deny the fear, but you see evidence that you might be more prepared than you feel.

Rehearsal of Calm Responses

Just as we rehearse for a performance, we can rehearse mental responses to anxiety triggers. Pick a situation that often sets off fear. Imagine it happening. Then imagine responding with calm words or actions. You do not have to picture everything going perfectly. Instead, focus on how you handle the fear in the moment.

This rehearsal can create a mental track that your mind follows in real life. When the situation appears, you may find it easier to slip into the calm response you have practiced. Over time, this builds confidence that you can choose how to react.

Noticing Progress as You Train the Mind

It is important to see the small steps you make. Maybe you catch yourself in a negative thought and pause before it becomes a big worry. That is progress. Maybe you quickly move from panic to a calming breath in a situation that used to freeze you. That is a real improvement.

We do not want fear or anxiety to vanish completely to call it a win. Each bit of progress shows that your mental training is working. The more you notice these gains, the more your mind learns that change is possible.

A Word About Professional Guidance

While these tools can help a great deal, sometimes fear and anxiety are strong enough to need professional help. Therapy can provide personalized methods, and medication can be an option if anxiety is severe. There is no shame in seeking extra support.

Think of these mind-training approaches as part of a larger set of resources. Therapists often use them as well, so learning them on your own can only help if you do decide to talk to a professional.

Conclusion of Chapter 7

Shaping a more peaceful mind involves noticing your **thought patterns**, questioning unhelpful beliefs, and practicing new ways of thinking. It is a gradual process that benefits from daily effort. Negative thoughts may still appear, but with these techniques, you can guide them rather than be controlled by them.

In the next chapter, **Chapter 8**, we will take these ideas further by talking about **building inner strength**. We will look at how self-worth, trust in our abilities, and a kinder view of ourselves can act as a solid base against fear. Chapter 8 will also explore the role of meaning and purpose in reducing anxiety. By merging the mental techniques from this chapter with the deeper sense of self we will discuss next, you will have an even stronger toolkit for facing whatever comes your way.

CHAPTER 8: BUILDING INNER STRENGTH

Introduction

When fear and anxiety show up, it can feel as though our inner support is missing. We might feel small or shaky, uncertain whether we can cope. Building **inner strength** means growing the sense that, no matter what happens, we have enough resilience and self-belief to stand our ground.

This chapter looks at how we can develop that inner support system. We will explore the meaning of **self-worth**, how to trust ourselves in times of doubt, and why having a sense of purpose can protect us from deep worry. We will also touch on the idea that compassion toward others can build compassion toward ourselves, further strengthening our core.

The Link Between Self-Worth and Fear

Self-worth is how we see our own value. When it is low, we may feel we do not deserve good things or that we are not capable of handling challenges. That insecurity can feed fear and anxiety. We might expect bad outcomes because we believe we cannot manage success.

On the other hand, a healthy sense of self-worth does not mean we think we are perfect. It means we accept ourselves, flaws included, and still see ourselves as worthy of care and respect. From this place, fear does not vanish, but it becomes more manageable. We trust we can handle problems or learn from them rather than seeing them as proof we are a failure.

Positive Self-Talk to Support Self-Worth

One step to build self-worth is to watch how we talk to ourselves. If that voice is always critical, it wears down our sense of value. We may find that fear takes over because the mind keeps telling us we are not good enough to cope.

Try small adjustments in self-talk. Instead of saying, "I am so stupid for not understanding this," say, "This is a tough thing to learn. It might take me a bit more time." Instead of saying, "I am a horrible person for feeling anxious," say, "I feel anxious, which happens sometimes, but I can find ways to ease it."

These shifts in self-talk do not ignore problems. They shift the blame from who we are to the situation or skill at hand. That helps protect our sense of worth when we face challenges.

Self-Esteem vs. Self-Worth

Self-esteem often depends on our achievements. We feel good about ourselves when we perform well, and we feel bad when we fail. Self-worth goes deeper. It means we value ourselves as human beings, regardless of success or failure.

When we put all our confidence in self-esteem, fear can spike if we are not at our best. We might think, "If I fail at this test or if I lose my job, I am nothing." True self-worth says, "I prefer to do well, but even if I fail, I am still a person with value."

This shift in how we see ourselves can greatly reduce fear. We no longer tie our identity to every win or loss. We can fail an exam or miss a promotion without it destroying our sense of who we are. That mental freedom takes a lot of the bite out of fear.

Trusting Yourself in Tough Times

Inner strength also comes from the sense that we can rely on ourselves when things get hard. This does not mean we never ask for help. It means we know, deep down, that we will do what we can, and that is often enough.

We build this trust by taking on small tasks and seeing them through. Each success, however small, is proof that we can follow through on a goal. Even if things do not go perfectly, we can note that we tried, adjusted, and survived. Over time, these experiences add up to a sense of trust in our own abilities.

The Power of Self-Efficacy

Self-efficacy is a term for the belief that we can complete the tasks or meet the challenges we face. People with high self-efficacy look at hard tasks as chances to learn rather than threats. Those with low self-efficacy might see the same tasks as proof they will fail.

To build self-efficacy, start with goals you can reach. Make them small and clear. As you achieve them, your brain learns that you can succeed in the things you set out to do. Next, raise the challenge bit by bit. This approach keeps you from being overwhelmed while still stretching your skills.

Facing Fear as an Act of Strength

It might sound strange, but each time we face fear directly, we strengthen our inner core. That does not mean we go looking for danger. It means when fear appears, we do not always run away. We take a moment, ground ourselves, and then decide on the next step.

Even if the step is small, it is still a move forward. Each time we do this, we show our mind that fear does not have the final say. We can live alongside it and still do what we must. Over time, this builds confidence that the presence of fear is not a sign we should give up.

The Role of Meaning in Handling Anxiety

When life feels empty or aimless, fear can take up more space. We might not see a reason to push through challenges if we do not have something meaningful to strive for. That is why having a sense of purpose or meaning can lower anxiety.

Purpose does not have to be grand. It could be caring for a loved one, building a skill, or contributing to a cause that matters to you. When we have a clear sense of why we do what we do, daily fears do not vanish, but they lose some of their power.

For instance, if you care deeply about helping homeless animals, you might accept some fear or discomfort while volunteering. The meaning of helping those animals is bigger than your immediate worry. This does not make fear fun, but it gives you a reason to face it.

Aligning Actions with Values

Another way to build inner strength is to align our actions with our core values. If honesty is important to us, we try to act honestly even when it is hard. If family is our top value, we look for ways to spend time with them or support them.

When our actions match our values, we feel more stable inside. We reduce inner conflict, which is often a breeding ground for anxiety. On the other hand, if we act against our values, we might feel guilt or shame, which can fuel fear.

By making choices that reflect who we want to be, we strengthen our sense of self. This leads to a steadier mind, because we know that whatever happens, we are living in line with what we hold dear.

The Body-Mind Connection in Inner Strength

We have touched on the body-mind link before, but it is worth noting again for inner strength. Taking care of our physical body with rest, good food, and some form of movement gives us a stronger base. When our body is rundown, our mind is more open to fear.

On top of that, certain activities, like gentle exercise or a calming stretch routine, can directly improve our mood and mental outlook. That boost can make it easier to believe in our own strength rather than seeing ourselves as helpless.

Supporting Others to Build Your Own Strength

It might sound backward, but helping others can also build your inner strength. When you support someone else through a tough time, you realize that humans can handle more than they think. Seeing a friend push through a problem can inspire you.

You also learn that your words or actions can make a difference in someone's life. That sense of being capable of giving support adds to your belief that you are not powerless. Fear shrinks when we feel we can do something meaningful, whether it is for ourselves or others.

Living with Uncertainty in a Balanced Way

Inner strength does not mean being sure about everything. It means learning to live with the fact that life is unpredictable, and that we can still act with calm and clarity in the face of that unknown.

Sometimes we try to find absolute certainty before we move forward. This is often impossible. Instead, with inner strength, we say, "I do not know how this will turn out, but I trust myself to handle whatever does happen." This approach shifts focus from controlling the outcome to trusting our ability to adapt.

Forgiving Ourselves and Learning

Many people hold onto regrets or guilt over past mistakes. This can weaken inner strength because it keeps us tied to a negative view of ourselves. Forgiveness is not about letting ourselves off the hook entirely. It is about accepting that we did the best we could at the time, or that we learned a lesson from what happened.

When we forgive ourselves, we free up mental space to face present challenges without carrying the weight of old failures. We can say, "I made a mistake, but I am using it to grow. I am still worthy of understanding and care." That sense of dignity feeds inner strength.

Building a Self-Image That Supports You

We all have a self-image—the view of who we are. Sometimes we pick up labels from others or from past events: "I am the shy one," or "I am the weak one." These labels might not be fair or accurate anymore, but we still carry them.

Part of building inner strength is looking at our self-image and asking, "Does this help me or harm me?" If the image is outdated or negative, we can adjust it. We might say, "I used to be shy, but I am learning to speak up more. I can be quiet at times, but I am not weak."

This does not mean we lie to ourselves. It means we allow the possibility that we have grown or that we have qualities we never noticed. By shaping a self-image that is realistic and kind, we give ourselves a better base to fight fear.

Accepting Emotions Without Letting Them Rule

Fear and anxiety are part of being human. Inner strength grows when we can accept those emotions without letting them decide our path. That might look like saying, "I feel scared right now, but I am still going to do what matters. I will bring my fear along, but I will not let it hold me back."

This acceptance can be combined with the techniques from Chapter 7. We notice the thought or emotion, label it, allow it to exist, and still move ahead with the choices that line up with our values. Over time, we see that fear loses some grip when we do not let it dictate our actions.

Grounding in the Present

We have discussed grounding methods before. They also help build inner strength. When we ground ourselves, we show that we can calm our body and mind in a stressful moment. Each time we do this, we strengthen our belief in our own ability to self-soothe.

Over many practices, that ability becomes part of our identity. We become someone who knows how to return to a steady place, even if fear tries to shake us. That is a big piece of inner strength: trusting that we can guide ourselves to safety from within.

Finding Supportive Connections

Inner strength does not mean we never need others. In fact, having supportive ties can boost our inner resources. Knowing that friends, family, or counselors are there if we stumble lets us take risks and face fears more bravely.

This does not make us dependent on them for every step. It just means we acknowledge that humans do better when they have a network of caring people around them. We can lean on that network when fear feels too big to handle alone, and in return, we can offer our help when they face their own worries.

The Role of Growth in Building Strength

Inner strength is not a single moment of realization. It is an ongoing process of growth. Each time you push through a fearful event, each time you learn a new skill, and each time you speak kindly to yourself, you add a bit more to your strength.

This growth is usually slow and sometimes uneven. We might feel strong one week and then slip back into doubt the next. That is normal. Growth can happen in bursts and pauses. The key is to keep going, trusting that every step adds up in the long run.

Practical Steps to Boost Inner Strength

1. **Set small tasks** you can manage, and complete them. This proves to yourself that you can follow through.
2. **Speak kindly** to yourself when fear appears. Remind yourself you have options and can handle discomfort.
3. **Reflect on achievements** you have made, no matter how small. This shows you that you do succeed at things.
4. **Help others** when possible, to see you can be of service and that your actions matter.
5. **Stay in line with your values**, so you feel solid about who you are.
6. **Allow failure** without letting it define your worth. Mistakes can be data for growth.
7. **Keep learning**—new ideas, new skills, new perspectives. This broadens your sense of what is possible.

Using these kinds of steps over weeks, months, and years can transform how you see yourself. Fear may still visit, but it will meet a stronger and more confident person than before.

Hope as a Part of Inner Strength

Hope is the belief that things can improve or that you can find meaning even in hard times. It does not mean ignoring pain or denying reality. It means trusting that life has more than just the problems you face right now.

When we have hope, we are more likely to try new solutions, ask for help, and see setbacks as temporary. This attitude itself is a form of inner strength because it pushes us to keep going rather than give up.

Conclusion of Chapter 8

Building **inner strength** involves growing self-worth, trusting in our ability to handle problems, and finding meaning that drives us forward. It is about shaping a stable sense of who we are, so fear and anxiety do not knock us down so easily. We can still feel afraid, but we stand up more quickly, knowing our core is solid.

This chapter closes **Part Four**, where we focused on the mind. We looked at techniques to create a more peaceful mental landscape and saw how a strong inner base can reduce fear. By blending the methods from Chapters 7 and 8, you can reshape your relationship with anxiety from within.

In the next section, **Part Five**, we will expand on these ideas by talking about **breaking patterns** that keep panic and fear cycles alive. We will look at practical steps to slow down panic and handle pressure in everyday life. The inner work from Part Four sets the stage for that practical work, giving you both the mindset and the skillset to move forward.

PART FIVE: BREAKING PATTERNS

You have learned about the nature of **fear** and **anxiety**, how to spot triggers, how to manage daily stress, and how to shape your mind toward greater calm. In this part, we will focus on breaking long-standing patterns that keep fear locked in place. We will look at steps to slow panic when it first appears, and we will explore ways to handle pressure in everyday living so that you do not fall back into old cycles.

This part includes two chapters:

- Chapter 9: Steps to Slow Down Panic
- Chapter 10: Handling Pressure in Daily Living

Both chapters will build on the methods you have learned so far. You will see how to take active measures when panic tries to grab hold of you, and you will learn how to avoid the traps that daily pressure can set for you. Breaking patterns is not a quick fix. It is an ongoing process of noticing what you do in tough moments and choosing a new way, again and again. By the end of these chapters, you should feel more prepared to face panic and pressure without being pulled into the old loops that keep fear and anxiety high.

CHAPTER 9: STEPS TO SLOW DOWN PANIC

Introduction

Panic is fear at its peak. It can feel like our body and mind spin out of control. We might think we are going to pass out, lose our sense of reality, or even die. These thoughts can multiply fast, feeding the panic until it feels too big to handle.

But panic does not come out of nowhere. There are signs that lead up to it. If we can spot those signs early, we can step in and slow the process before it becomes a full-scale panic attack. In this chapter, we will look at how panic forms, why certain habits keep it going, and what specific steps you can take to break that cycle.

How Panic Builds

A panic attack often begins with a sudden wave of fear or worry. Maybe you have a stressful thought, see something that triggers a memory of danger, or feel a strange sensation in your body. This spark sets off the "fight or flight" system, sending adrenaline through your bloodstream. Your heart might race, your breathing may become short, and you might sweat or feel dizzy.

Next, your mind notices these body changes and starts to interpret them in a fearful way. You might think, "I am losing control," or "This feeling will never end." These thoughts add to your anxiety, which makes your symptoms worse. It becomes a loop: body symptoms trigger scary thoughts, which fuel more symptoms.

If nothing interrupts this loop, the fear can ramp up until it feels overwhelming. That is when we might call it a full-blown panic attack. It does not last forever, but in the moment, it can seem endless.

Common Triggers for Panic

- **Health worries**: A sudden pain or shortness of breath can make you think you have a serious illness or are about to collapse.
- **Fear of losing control**: Some people feel panic when they cannot leave a situation easily (like being stuck on a busy train).
- **Old memories**: Trauma or upsetting past events can be stored in the body. A sight, sound, or smell might bring them back, sparking panic.
- **Intense stress**: Ongoing tension, whether from work, family, or finances, can wear you down until a small event tips you into panic mode.
- **Unclear triggers**: Sometimes, panic can feel like it comes "out of the blue," but there is often a hidden chain of thoughts or small events leading up to it.

Early Signs of Rising Panic

Before panic hits full force, many people notice subtle clues:

- **Tightness in the chest**: It may feel like it is hard to breathe, or your heart is pounding harder than normal.
- **Tingling** or numbness in your hands or face.
- **Racing thoughts**: A sudden flood of worries.
- **Restlessness**: Feeling unable to sit still.
- **Sense of dread**: An odd feeling that something terrible is about to happen.

Spotting these signs early is key. If you can catch them, you have a window of time to use the steps below to slow your panic.

Step 1: Acknowledge the Oncoming Panic

One of the first ways to slow panic is to say, "I notice the signs of panic starting." This might sound simple, but it helps you shift from being lost in the feeling to observing it. You are telling yourself, "I see what is happening, and I know this is a panic response."

If you feel your heart racing or your hands shaking, you can name it: "There is my fast heartbeat. My hands are shaky." By labeling the signs, you bring the thinking part of your brain into the picture. This helps put a small brake on the runaway fear.

Step 2: Use a Grounding Method Right Away

Once you spot panic rising, step into a grounding method. One you might recall is the **five senses** approach. For example:

1. Look for **five** things around you that you can see.
2. Notice **four** things you can feel (such as the texture of your clothes or the chair under you).
3. Listen for **three** sounds in your area.
4. Become aware of **two** things you can smell.
5. Note **one** thing you can taste (or recall a taste you like).

Doing this forces your mind to switch from fearful thoughts to concrete details. It reminds you that you are here in the present. Panic often wants to drag you into a mental storm. Grounding pulls you back to what is real.

Step 3: Slow Your Breathing

When panic hits, breathing tends to speed up, causing dizziness or a sense of choking. You can slow this by breathing in and out at a steady pace. For instance, try inhaling for four counts, hold for a brief moment, then exhale for four counts. If four is too long or too short, find a count that fits your body's natural pace, but keep it even.

While you breathe, focus on feeling the air move in and out. You might rest a hand on your lower belly to sense it rising and falling. Remind yourself that the worst part of panic often comes from shallow, fast breathing. By slowing your breath, you send a signal that can help calm the adrenaline rush.

Step 4: Remind Yourself That Panic Is Temporary

When panic surges, it can feel like it will last forever. But panic attacks usually peak within a few minutes and then start to ease. Telling yourself this fact can lessen the dread. Some people say, "This is just a surge of fear. It will pass soon."

Panic is like a wave. It rises, hits a crest, and then begins to fall. If you ride the wave instead of fighting it, you often find it is not as endless as it seems. Of course, it can still be uncomfortable, but remembering that it is time-limited helps you keep a sense of control.

Step 5: Check for Thought Distortions

During panic, thoughts become frantic. You might think, "I am dying," or "I will lose my mind." These are typical **catastrophic** ideas that fuel panic. Ask yourself, "Is there proof that this is true, or am I letting the panic exaggerate things?"

You do not have to debate every thought in detail—sometimes, just recognizing it is panic talking can help. For instance, you might say, "I feel like I am dying, but I have had panic attacks before and I survived. My heart is pounding, but that does not mean it will stop."

Step 6: Change the Setting, If Possible

If you are in a place that is adding to your panic—maybe a crowded area or a stuffy room—moving to a slightly calmer spot can help. This does not mean fleeing the situation entirely if that is not wise. It might just mean stepping outside for fresh air or finding a quiet corner to practice your slow breathing.

If moving is not an option, you can still make small changes. Adjust your posture, or turn your body away from a source of stress. Even closing your eyes for a moment (if it feels safe) can reduce visual overload and help you reset.

Step 7: Use Simple Self-Talk

When panic flares, your mind may be yelling all kinds of alarming things. Counter this with short, clear phrases. Examples:

- "I can be afraid, but I am not in true danger right now."
- "These feelings are scary, but they are not harmful."
- "I know panic passes. I am okay."

Repeat these like a mantra. The goal is to replace the flood of panic thoughts with steady reminders of the truth.

Step 8: Bring in a Calming Item or Image

Some people find it helpful to keep a small item with them for moments of panic, like a smooth pebble, a piece of fabric, or a photo that brings calm. Touching or looking at this item can bring a sense of safety or comfort.

If you do not have a physical item, you can hold a mental image: a calm beach or a warm room you like. Recall the details of that place. This can work like a mini vacation for your mind during the peak of panic.

Step 9: Practice Tolerating Discomfort

Panic attacks are highly uncomfortable. One long-term way to reduce them is to build a tolerance for discomfort. This does not mean you force yourself into terror, but rather that you accept you can handle some level of fear without it destroying you.

If you feel the start of panic, remind yourself you can let the feeling rise and still be safe. Your heart might pound, but it will not burst. Your hands might tremble, but they will not fail you. By staying with the sensation, you teach your body and mind that panic is not the end of the world.

Step 10: Review What Worked Afterward

When the panic eases, take a moment to look back. Which steps helped you the most? Were there signs you spotted early? Did any coping method stand out? Write these things down or mentally note them.

Building this record helps you become more skilled at handling panic each time. It also reassures you that you can live through a panic attack and come out the other side. Over time, this process can reduce the overall fear of panic itself.

Avoiding the Fear of Fear

A major problem that can worsen panic is the fear of having another panic attack. You might worry so much about panic that you keep yourself in a stressed state. This is sometimes called **anticipatory anxiety**.

It is natural to feel nervous about more panic, but try to keep in mind that fearing the fear often creates more tension. Instead, remind yourself that if another panic attack comes, you have tools to handle it. You cannot stop all fear from showing up, but you can guide it once it is there.

Long-Term Steps to Reduce Panic

While the above steps can help in the moment, long-term changes also matter. Getting enough rest, eating balanced meals, and having a daily routine of gentle movement or short walks can stabilize your body. Using the mental skills from earlier chapters can keep your overall anxiety level lower, making panic less likely to strike out of the blue.

Some people also seek therapy specifically for panic. Treatments like cognitive-behavioral approaches or specialized programs can help you face the fear of panic in a structured way. If your panic attacks feel too intense to manage alone, there is no shame in getting that extra support.

Gradual Exposure to Panic Triggers

If certain places or situations trigger panic—such as driving on highways, being in crowded malls, or riding elevators—you might try a gradual exposure plan. You break the situation into smaller steps. For instance, if you fear driving on freeways, you might:

1. Sit in your parked car on the driveway and practice calming your mind.
2. Drive around your neighborhood for a short time.
3. Drive on a quiet road that leads to a freeway entrance but do not enter it yet.
4. Enter the freeway for one exit and then get off.
5. Slowly extend the distance as you feel more comfortable.

At each step, you use your coping tools. This teaches your body and mind that while the situation may bring discomfort, you can manage it without panicking. Over time, the trigger holds less power.

Helping Loved Ones Understand

When people around you do not understand panic attacks, they might say unhelpful things like, "Just relax," or "It is all in your head." It can help to explain to them that panic is a real physical and mental event. Give them an idea of how they can help, like offering calm words or giving you space to use your grounding methods.

We cannot control how others respond, but we can try to educate them so they do not add more stress. Let them know that saying, "You will be okay, take your time" can be far more helpful than, "Stop overreacting."

Panic vs. Ongoing Anxiety

Panic attacks are intense bursts of fear, but many people also experience a steady level of anxiety day to day. These two problems can feed each other. If you are already anxious, you might be more prone to panic. If you have had a panic attack recently, you might remain on alert, raising your general anxiety.

The steps in earlier chapters—like questioning negative thoughts, building routines, or practicing steady relaxation—can help with both. By lowering your overall tension, you reduce the chance that a small spark will turn into a big panic storm.

A Reminder That You Are Not Alone

Millions of people experience panic attacks. You may feel isolated, but you are not. Support groups, online forums, or therapy settings can connect you with others who deal with the same challenge. Sharing tips and stories (in a balanced way, without dwelling on fear) can give you fresh hope and insights.

Conclusion of Chapter 9

Panic attacks can feel overpowering, but they do not have to run your life. By noticing early signs, using grounding and breathing methods, and challenging extreme thoughts, you can slow panic's grip. It may take practice, but each time you face a panic surge, you learn more about how to guide your mind and body toward calm.

In the next chapter, **Chapter 10**, we will turn our attention to handling daily pressure. It is not just moments of panic that need attention—ongoing stress can build a background of worry that increases the chance of panic in the first place. Learning how to manage daily demands without sliding into old fear patterns is key. These two chapters together will help you break the cycles that keep anxiety high, giving you more freedom to live a calmer life.

CHAPTER 10: HANDLING PRESSURE IN DAILY LIVING

Introduction

While panic attacks are dramatic events, much of our fear and anxiety can also come from constant, smaller sources of pressure in daily life. We may face deadlines at work, conflicts at home, or a general sense that we are never doing enough. These pressures can become so normal that we hardly notice them—until we are overwhelmed.

In this chapter, we will look at how to handle daily demands in a way that reduces fear and anxiety. This includes practical methods for planning tasks, dealing with conflicts, setting personal limits, and finding moments of rest. By learning to handle everyday stress in a steady manner, we lower the risk of reaching a breaking point.

Recognizing Hidden Sources of Pressure

Many pressures do not appear as big crises. They might be small things that add up:

- **Too many tasks**: Trying to juggle work, family, chores, and personal projects all at once.
- **Emotional strains**: Worrying about a friend in trouble or feeling guilt about something we said.
- **Perfectionism**: Holding ourselves to a standard that is impossible to meet.
- **Fear of letting people down**: Agreeing to tasks we do not have time for.
- **Social pressures**: Feeling we must always be available or respond quickly to every message.

Over time, these can drain our energy. We might not call it anxiety, but our body can stay on alert, ready for a problem.

Step 1: List Out Your Pressures

A good first step is to write down the main sources of daily pressure. Seeing them on paper can bring clarity. You might list:

- Tasks you do each day (including small chores).
- Emotional concerns (like conflicts with friends or family).
- Financial worries (bills, debts, saving plans).
- Personal expectations (fitness goals, skill-building, etc.).

Doing this might feel overwhelming at first, but it helps you see what you are carrying. Many people are surprised to discover how many small or medium concerns are weighing on them.

Step 2: Sort the Pressures by Priority

Not all items on your list are equally urgent. Sort them into groups like "must do now," "can wait," or "would be nice, but not crucial." This basic sorting helps you focus on what truly needs your attention.

Sometimes we treat every task as a crisis, which raises our stress level. By choosing what comes first, we place some order on the chaos. This alone can reduce anxiety because we no longer feel like everything is equally urgent.

Step 3: Plan Your Day with Realistic Blocks of Time

Instead of trying to handle everything at once, set clear blocks of time for each group of tasks. Maybe you decide that from 9 AM to 10 AM you work on a specific report, from 10 AM to 10:15 AM you take a break, then from 10:15 AM to 11 AM you answer emails. By creating a plan, you help your mind settle.

Make sure to include short breaks, even if it is just a few minutes to stand and stretch. These pauses help prevent mental overload. The body and mind need brief resets to perform well over the day.

Step 4: Learn to Say "No" More Often

If you are someone who hates letting people down, you might say "yes" to every request. This can lead to an overflow of tasks and make daily pressure unmanageable. While it is good to be helpful, it is not good to reach a point of constant stress.

Saying "no" or "not now" can be hard. But if you take on too much, you risk burning out and not doing a good job on anything. You can start by politely declining smaller requests or asking if the task can wait. Over time, people around you learn to respect your limits.

Step 5: Watch Out for Perfectionism

Perfectionism can keep you under constant tension. You might spend far too long on details that do not matter much or avoid completing tasks because you fear they will not be perfect. This can increase anxiety and reduce what you get done.

Try to set goals that are "good enough" rather than perfect. If you can deliver a decent piece of work on time, that might be better than striving for perfection and never finishing. It helps to remind yourself that small mistakes are normal and can often be fixed later if needed.

Step 6: Reduce Decision Fatigue

Making too many decisions in a day can wear down your ability to handle stress. One way to lower decision fatigue is to set simple routines. For example, you might plan your meals ahead of time or choose which days you do certain chores. You remove the need to decide on these things daily.

Another tip is to limit choices for tasks that do not matter much. If you spend a lot of time picking clothes, consider keeping a simpler wardrobe or deciding the night before. Small changes like this can free up mental space for more important concerns.

Step 7: Use Short Pauses to Check In

Pressure can build slowly throughout the day. You can counter this by taking short "check-in" breaks. Every hour or two, pause for 30 seconds (if possible) and ask: "How am I feeling? Is my breathing tense? Am I rushing?"

If you notice tension, take a slow breath, drop your shoulders, and reset. These small resets keep stress from growing unnoticed until you are in panic mode. They also help you respond more calmly to surprises.

Step 8: Handle Conflict Early and Respectfully

Conflicts with coworkers, friends, or family can create a lingering sense of dread. We might put off talking about a problem, hoping it goes away. In many cases, it does not; it just festers.

When a conflict arises, try to address it sooner rather than later, and do so respectfully. That might mean explaining your feelings calmly, asking for the other person's view, and looking for a solution that benefits both sides if possible. Even if it is an uncomfortable talk, handling it can remove a huge source of daily pressure.

Step 9: Limit Overexposure to News or Social Media

Many people feel added stress from constant news or social media. While staying informed is good, a nonstop flood of negativity can heighten anxiety. Consider setting specific times to check news or social feeds, rather than doing it all day.

If certain sites or channels constantly make you feel upset, see if you can cut them out or reduce them. Remind yourself that you do not need to read every headline as it breaks. When you control your intake, you reduce the mental overload that fuels daily pressure.

Step 10: Practice Clear Communication

Misunderstandings can create extra stress. Learning to say what you need or what you are concerned about in a calm, direct way can prevent confusion. If we speak vaguely or assume others know what we mean, small issues can grow into big worries.

For example, if you have a heavy workload, let your boss know you need more time or help. If a friend keeps texting you late at night, kindly explain you need that time to rest. Clarity can save both sides a lot of anxiety.

Step 11: Rotate Tasks or Vary Your Day

Doing the same kind of task for too long can lead to mental fatigue. If possible, switch between different types of work. For instance, after doing one hour of computer-based tasks, spend 15 minutes tidying your workspace or doing something more hands-on.

Varying tasks can refresh your mind and keep pressure from mounting in one area. Of course, not every job allows total flexibility, but see if you can create small shifts. Even a walk to refill water or a few stretches at your desk can break the monotony.

Step 12: Lean on Support Systems

Do not try to handle all daily pressures alone. If you have friends, family, or coworkers who can share the load, let them. This might mean dividing chores at home, delegating tasks at work, or simply talking about stress with someone who will listen.

Support systems are not just for crises; they can help keep everyday stress in check. By staying connected with people you trust, you can often spot issues before they turn into bigger problems.

Step 13: Plan for Breaks and Fun Activities

If your day is all work and no rest, you may slide into a cycle of tension. Plan small moments of fun or relaxation. This could be a hobby, a short call with a friend, or a favorite piece of music during lunch.

These little "joy breaks" remind you that life is not just about tasks and deadlines. They also let your mind unwind, which can renew your energy for the next challenge.

Step 14: Set Boundaries with Technology

Smartphones and computers can blur the line between work and personal life. We may feel we must respond to emails or messages at all hours. This constant availability increases daily pressure.

Try setting certain hours when you do not check work messages, or create a habit of turning off notifications for certain apps after a set time. It might feel odd at first, but it can help you regain a sense of balance.

Step 15: Watch for Avoidance

Sometimes, daily pressure can lead us to avoid tasks out of fear or dread. But avoidance often doubles the stress later on, because the task still has to be done. If you sense you are putting something off, ask yourself why. Are you afraid you will fail? Is it confusing to start?

Break the task into smaller steps or seek help if needed. Even if you take one small action on it, that can reduce the looming dread. Overcoming avoidance is a key part of preventing small pressures from building into larger anxiety.

Step 16: Check In with Your Physical Health

Fatigue, poor eating habits, or lack of physical activity can make daily pressures harder to handle. If you are running on little sleep or skipping meals, you are more prone to feeling overwhelmed.

Try to get enough rest, aim for balanced meals, and find some gentle movement each day. Small improvements in physical health can make a big difference in how you handle mental stress.

Step 17: Practice Quick Relaxation

When a task is stressful, take a minute to close your eyes (if you can) and breathe slowly. Picture the tension leaving your body with each exhale. This tiny pause can help you reset and approach the task with a clearer mind.

If you do this regularly, you might notice that even tough tasks feel a bit more doable. You are training yourself to stay calmer under pressure rather than letting it spike your anxiety.

Step 18: Keep an Eye on Negative Self-Talk

When the day is busy, negative thoughts can slip in without notice. You might call yourself lazy or incompetent if you fall behind schedule, or you might blame yourself for every problem that appears. This kind of self-talk increases the sense of pressure.

Each time you catch a negative statement in your mind, see if you can replace it with a balanced thought: "I have many tasks today, but I am doing my best," or "I am behind schedule, but I will ask for help or revise my plan."

Step 19: Learn From Bad Days

Some days, pressure will boil over despite your efforts. Rather than beating yourself up, see what you can learn. Did you try to do too much? Did you forget to say "no" to certain tasks? Did you skip your breaks?

By spotting patterns, you can make changes so future days go more smoothly. Even a tough day can be useful if it shows where your plan might need adjusting.

Step 20: Maintain a Flexible Mindset

Life is unpredictable. Even the best plans can get derailed by a surprise phone call or a sudden request from your boss. Try to keep a flexible mindset: "I will do what I can with the time and energy I have, and if something changes, I will adapt."

This attitude reduces the shock when things do not go as planned. Flexibility is key to staying steady when daily pressure ramps up. It also helps you avoid turning small setbacks into huge stressors.

Balancing Responsibility and Self-Care

Handling daily pressure means finding a balance between meeting obligations and taking care of yourself. Both matter. If you ignore your responsibilities, you might feel guilt and stress pile up later. If you ignore self-care, you might burn out.

Think of balance as a moving target. Some days, you might focus more on tasks. Other days, you might need extra rest or personal time. The goal is not a perfect 50-50 split every day, but an overall sense that both areas get attention.

Avoid Comparing Yourself to Others

Seeing others who seem to handle a dozen tasks with ease can make you feel inadequate. But you do not know their full story. They might be struggling in ways you cannot see. Comparison often leads to unnecessary pressure and shame.

Focus on your own pace and progress. Ask yourself if you are getting better at handling stress than you were last month or last year. That is a more useful measure than comparing yourself to someone else's outside image.

Combining These Steps with Earlier Skills

Remember the breathing methods, grounding practices, and thought-challenging approaches from past chapters. They can be used whenever daily pressure feels like it is hitting a danger level. If you notice tension rising in the middle of a busy day, pause for some slow breathing or question a negative assumption.

These small interventions can prevent you from sliding into panic or chronic worry. They act like brakes on a rolling train. You do not have to wait for the train to get to top speed before you try to slow it down.

Conclusion of Chapter 10

Handling pressure in daily living is about noticing the tasks and demands that surround you, creating a plan to handle them, and using steady skills to keep stress at bay. By making small shifts—such as setting boundaries, staying flexible, and doing quick resets—you can keep daily strain from turning into a larger wave of anxiety or panic.

This completes **Part Five**, where we looked at how to break patterns of panic and manage everyday pressure. In Chapter 9, we focused on steps to slow down panic when it starts. In Chapter 10, we explored ways to prevent constant stress from piling up.

When you blend these steps with the inner skills you have developed so far, you build a strong defense against fear. You may still face challenges, but you are less likely to fall back into old cycles of panic or worry.

PART SIX: GROWING BETTER HABITS

You have now explored many ideas for handling **fear** and **anxiety**. Parts One through Five showed you how to spot these feelings, use daily tools to calm them, shape your thoughts in a healthier way, and break old patterns that keep panic and stress going. In **Part Six**, we will look at **growing better habits** that support a calmer life in the long run.

Chapter 11 will show how to find the right **support system**, both in personal ties and in professional help, and how to lean on others in a way that strengthens your own ability to cope. **Chapter 12** will focus on **challenging unhelpful thoughts**, offering new ways to question negative beliefs that keep fear strong. By the end of these chapters, you will have a clearer sense of how to weave these habits into your daily life so that fear and anxiety lose their grip over time.

CHAPTER 11: FINDING THE RIGHT SUPPORT SYSTEM

Introduction

Fear and anxiety can grow when we feel cut off from others. Even if we work hard on our own, it can be hard to keep calm if we lack supportive voices around us. A strong support system can ease our stress, share our burdens, and remind us that we are not alone. It can come from friends, family, or professionals like counselors. It can also come from groups or communities, both online and in person.

This chapter will help you see how to build and keep a support system that meets your needs. We will talk about how to spot people who truly help, how to talk to them about your fears, and how to draw healthy boundaries if needed. We will also look at when and how to seek more direct professional help.

Why Support Matters for Fear and Anxiety

When we feel anxious or afraid, our minds can trick us into thinking no one would care or understand. We might keep our worries hidden, fearing judgment. But support breaks that isolation. Sharing a fear with someone we trust can make it less heavy, even if the fear itself does not vanish right away.

Research also shows that people with good social ties tend to handle stress better. They can calm themselves more quickly and bounce back sooner from setbacks. Talking with others can lower levels of stress chemicals in our bodies. It can also give us new ideas or strategies we might not have thought of alone.

Types of Support

1. **Emotional support**: This comes from people who can listen to you without harsh judgment, offer comfort, and show you genuine concern. They might not have all the answers, but their empathy can be a soothing force.
2. **Practical support**: Some people help us by taking on tasks we find too stressful or by guiding us through tricky steps. They might give rides to appointments, help with chores, or share resources that reduce daily stress.
3. **Professional support**: Therapists, counselors, and mental health workers fit here. They have training to help you unpack deep worries, form new coping habits, or manage strong symptoms of anxiety.
4. **Community support**: This can be found in groups that share a common concern, like a local meetup or an online forum. Talking to others who face similar fears can help you feel less alone.

How to Spot True Helpers

Not everyone who offers help is truly supportive. Some people may judge you, minimize your feelings, or drain your energy. To find real helpers, look for these signs:

- They listen closely and do not rush to give advice before hearing you out.

- They do not mock or shame you for your fears.
- They respect your privacy and do not share your personal issues without permission.
- They encourage healthy coping, rather than pushing quick fixes or ignoring your feelings.

You might already know someone like this in your circle—maybe a friend who has been patient with you, or a relative who has always been kind when you are down. Those are the ties worth nurturing.

Reaching Out to Potential Supporters

Sometimes, we wait for people to notice our struggles and reach out first. But they might not realize how serious our worries are. Taking the step to ask for support can feel scary, but it can also deepen trust.

You could start by saying something like, "I have been feeling quite anxious lately and could use someone to talk with. Would you be able to lend an ear?" If they seem open, share a bit more about what you are going through. The goal is not to dump every worry on them at once. Instead, give them a chance to hear you at a steady pace and respond.

Creating a Support Network, Not Just One Person

Relying on only one person for all help can put too much weight on that tie. It can also limit the variety of support you get. Different people might be better at different things. One friend might be a great listener, while another is good at offering practical advice. A therapist can guide you with expert knowledge, while an online community might give a sense of belonging to a larger group of people who understand.

Think of building a **network** of support. This can include:

- One or two close friends or family members you trust with your deeper feelings.
- A professional you can see regularly if anxiety is intense or long-lasting.
- A group, in person or online, where you can exchange ideas with people who have similar goals.

By having more than one source, you reduce the load on any single person and ensure you have support in different areas of life.

Communicating Your Limits and Needs

A support system works best when there is clear communication. Let people know what is helpful and what is not. For example, you might say, "It helps when you just listen before suggesting solutions," or "I really appreciate it when you check in once in a while." If someone is pushing too hard or dismissing your feelings, gently tell them that it makes you more anxious instead of calm.

Communication also means setting limits if needed. If a friend has a habit of turning every talk into their own problems, you can respectfully say, "I value our talks, but I also need time to work through my own fears. Is it okay if I share what is on my mind first?" This way, you keep the bond healthy without feeling overshadowed.

Handling Negative Responses

Not everyone will respond kindly to your request for help. Some might roll their eyes, say you are overreacting, or accuse you of seeking attention. While this can hurt, remember that it says more about them than about your worth.

If you face a negative reaction, do not assume it means you cannot get support. It may just mean that person is not able to help in the way you need. You can still look for support elsewhere. If the negativity is severe, you might consider limiting contact with that person, especially in moments when your anxiety is high.

Building Support in New Places

If you do not have close people you can trust or if you live in a place where you feel alone, you can look for support groups or communities focused on anxiety and stress. Many towns have local groups that meet to talk about coping methods. If you cannot find one nearby, there are often online forums or groups dedicated to mental wellness.

When joining an online group, watch for spaces that feel safe and moderated. Some forums are full of panic-driven posts that might make your anxiety worse.

Look for groups with supportive, respectful members who share ideas, not just fear.

Balancing Support with Independence

While support is key, it does not mean we rely on others for every step. We still need to keep up with our own coping methods—like breathing exercises, thought-challenging, or daily routines. Support should add to our ability to handle fear, not replace it. We do not want to depend so heavily on others that we cannot function alone.

Think of support as an added resource. You do your work each day to manage anxiety, but sometimes you need a helping hand or a kind ear. That balance keeps you growing stronger while still gaining the benefits of being connected with others.

Understanding When Professional Help Is Needed

In some cases, fear and anxiety might be more than friends or family can help you manage. If you find your daily functioning severely limited—like you cannot get out of bed, go to work, or keep up with basic tasks—it might be time to talk with a therapist or counselor. They can give structured guidance, use tested methods, and track your progress over time.

Professional help can also be an option if your anxiety is linked to a deeper issue like trauma, or if it triggers habits that are harmful to your health. Therapists are trained to handle these situations with specific strategies. They can also refer you to medical help if you might need medication.

Considering Group Sessions or Workshops

Some communities offer workshops or group sessions where people learn coping skills together. A trained leader may teach techniques like slow breathing, grounding, or thought-challenging in a class setting. Attending such a group can give you two forms of help: the chance to learn new methods and the chance to meet others who understand what you are facing.

Group sessions can also be more affordable than individual therapy in many places. You might check with local community centers, mental health clinics, or online directories to find such options.

Keeping an Eye on Your Online Interactions

Online communication can be a two-sided coin. It can bring wonderful support from people worldwide, but it can also lead to negativity or misinformation if you land in the wrong place. Choose your online interactions with care. Notice how a certain forum or social media group makes you feel over time. If you leave the conversation more anxious than before, it might not be the right fit.

You can also form smaller online chat groups with a few trusted friends if a large forum feels too public. This private setting might allow more honest sharing without the fear of being judged by strangers.

Practical Ways Friends Can Help

Sometimes friends or family want to help but do not know how. You can guide them with specific tasks:

- Asking them to join you in a calming walk when you feel on edge.
- Requesting a check-in phone call at a certain time each week.
- Letting them know you might text them a short message if you feel panic rising.
- Suggesting activities that reduce stress, like sitting quietly, doing a simple craft together, or watching a gentle show.

By giving concrete ideas, you help them help you. It also keeps you from feeling disappointed if they do not offer the exact type of support you need.

When Loved Ones Disagree with Your Approach

Sometimes family or friends have strong opinions about mental health. They might say things like, "You just need to snap out of it," or "Therapy is a waste of time," if they have not learned much about anxiety. This can create tension if you are trying to practice coping methods or seek counseling.

In these cases, it can help to calmly explain what you are doing and why it matters. You might say, "I am working on reducing my anxiety with some proven methods. I need you to respect that." If they keep pushing, you may have to limit how much you share with them about your progress. Focus instead on those who do support you.

Building a Team Mindset at Home

If you live with others, you can create a mini teamwork approach. For instance, let them know what triggers your anxiety and ask for small tweaks. Maybe loud noise after 10 PM spikes your stress, so you ask if they can wear headphones. Or you feel uneasy if the house is always messy, so you suggest a shared cleaning schedule.

When everyone feels like part of the solution rather than the cause of the problem, home life can become calmer. Even small steps, like sharing cooking tasks or planning a nightly quiet time, can lessen stress and ease fear.

Checking in with Yourself Before and After Reaching Out

Each time you plan to share your worries with someone, it might help to pause and check how you feel before the talk. Notice if you feel shame, fear, or hope. Then, after the talk, notice again how you feel. Do you feel lighter, calmer, or do you feel more stressed?

This simple check can help you see which ties are genuinely helpful. If you find that talking to a certain person often leaves you feeling worse, it does not mean they are a bad person. But it might mean they are not the right source of support for your anxiety concerns. You can still enjoy other parts of your bond without expecting them to help with your fears.

Supporting Others in Return

Healthy support goes both ways. While your fear and anxiety might feel central right now, you can still be a good listener when others want to share something. Even a small act, like sending a text to see how someone is doing, can keep the bond balanced. This does not mean you ignore your own needs, but rather that you also show care in the ways you are able to handle.

Being supportive to others can actually lift your own mood and remind you that everyone faces challenges. It is not all on you. This sense of shared humanity can make your worries feel a bit less isolating.

The Lasting Effects of a Good Support System

When you have people to lean on, it becomes easier to take on daily stresses, face triggers, and even experiment with new coping methods. You feel less alone, which can reduce the dread that fuels anxiety. Over time, these supportive ties can help you maintain the progress you have made in the earlier parts of this book.

A good support system does not end fear, but it can keep it in perspective. You learn that fear is just one part of life, not the whole story, and that you have people in your corner. That knowledge can be a strong force against the pull of anxiety.

Conclusion of Chapter 11

Finding and keeping the right support system is a major step toward reducing **fear** and **anxiety**. By reaching out, setting clear expectations, and recognizing who can genuinely help, you build a network that makes tough days more manageable. Support should not replace your own efforts, but it can lift you when your personal resources feel low.

In **Chapter 12**, we will look at the next part of growing better habits: **challenging unhelpful thoughts**. We touched on this topic in earlier chapters, but now we will go further into methods that help you catch and rework thoughts that feed anxiety. By shaping your mindset and leaning on your support system, you can keep fear from ruling your choices in daily life.

CHAPTER 12: CHALLENGING UNHELPFUL THOUGHTS

Introduction

We have already explored how thoughts affect our feelings and actions. Now we will go deeper into methods for spotting and transforming **unhelpful thoughts**. These thoughts might be exaggerated, negative, or based on old beliefs that do not reflect reality. They can fuel anxiety by painting the world as a place of constant danger or by telling us we are not able to cope.

In this chapter, we will examine specific strategies to question and reshape those thoughts. We will also look at how to do this in a balanced way—without jumping to forced positivity. The aim is to see things more accurately, which can lower fear and help you make better choices.

Signs of Unhelpful Thoughts

Unhelpful thoughts can show up in many forms, such as:

- **Catastrophic thinking**: Always expecting the worst to happen.
- **Harsh self-criticism**: Calling yourself names or telling yourself you cannot do anything right.
- **Fortune telling**: Acting as though you can predict negative outcomes without real proof.
- **Mind reading**: Believing you know what others think, usually assuming they judge you harshly.
- **All-or-nothing**: Seeing events or performance as complete success or total failure, with nothing in between.

When you notice yourself feeling a strong surge of anxiety, pause and ask, "What thought did I just have?" That question alone can reveal these unhelpful patterns.

Step 1: Write Down the Thought

A simple but effective way to challenge a thought is to write it down. This shifts it from your mind onto paper, making it easier to observe. For instance, if you feel anxious about an upcoming work presentation, you might note:

- **Situation**: Giving a presentation tomorrow.
- **Anxious Thought**: "I will embarrass myself and get fired."

Putting it in black and white can clarify how extreme the worry might be.

Step 2: Ask for Evidence

Next, ask yourself: "What is the proof that this will happen, and what is the proof that it might not happen?" For the example above:

- **Proof it might happen**: Maybe you have stumbled over words in the past, or you have not practiced enough.
- **Proof it might not**: Perhaps you have given other presentations that went okay, or your boss has not fired people over small mistakes.

Looking at both sides can bring balance. Unhelpful thoughts often focus only on the negative side.

Step 3: Look for Alternative Views

Once you see the facts, consider other ways to see the situation. Maybe instead of "I will embarrass myself and get fired," you can say, "I might be nervous, but I can prepare, and even if I stumble, it will likely be fine in the end." This new view does not deny the possibility of making mistakes. It just places them in a more realistic context.

Step 4: Check If You Are "Fortune Telling"

Many anxious thoughts assume the future with great certainty. We might say, "I know I will fail," or "They will definitely laugh at me." But the truth is we do not know the future. If you catch yourself using absolute words like **will** or **definitely** about future events, that is a sign you might be guessing the worst without facts.

Try changing that language to something more open, like, "It is possible that things might go worse than I hope, but it is also possible they might turn out okay." By giving space to the unknown, you stop locking yourself into a negative fate.

Step 5: Practice "Could vs. Will" Language

When we say "I could lose my job," it leaves room for other outcomes. When we say "I will lose my job," it feels locked in stone. By swapping "will" for "could," we reduce the absolute sense of doom. This might seem like a small language shift, but it can ease a lot of pressure.

Step 6: Scale the Problem

Another method is to ask, "On a scale of 1 to 10, how bad would this really be?" People in the grip of anxiety might treat every risk as a 10. But if you reflect, you might find that some outcomes are more like a 4 or 5—unpleasant, but not devastating.

You can also do the same with your ability to cope: "On a scale of 1 to 10, how able am I to manage this if it happens?" You might discover that your ability is higher than you first assumed, which takes away some of fear's power.

Step 7: Reverse the Perspective

Sometimes, we can challenge thoughts by imagining a friend came to us with the same worry. How would we respond to them? Usually, we would be kinder than we are to ourselves. We might point out that they have succeeded before or that the worst case is not likely. By reversing the perspective, we see our own situation in a more balanced light.

Step 8: Keep It Real, Not Perfect

Challenging unhelpful thoughts does not mean forcing yourself to think everything is wonderful. It is about seeing reality more clearly. If you are worried about an exam, the balanced view might be: "I am nervous and I might not get the highest score, but I have studied and I can do my best." That is not blind positivity. It is a realistic statement that lowers panic.

Step 9: Limit Time Spent on "What-Ifs"

If you find yourself stuck on endless "what-if" questions, set aside a brief period each day to think them through. For example, let yourself worry for 10 minutes at lunch. When the "what-ifs" appear at another time, gently remind yourself you have a "worry time" set aside. Over days or weeks, this can reduce constant rumination.

Step 10: Be Aware of Labels

We often label ourselves with words like "loser," "failure," or "coward." These labels can trap us into seeing our identity as fixed. If you catch yourself using these terms, ask whether they are fair or if they are just unhelpful name-calling. Even if you failed at something, it does not mean you are always a failure. Notice how big the label is and see if you can replace it with a more accurate phrase, like "I am someone who made a mistake this time."

Step 11: Consider the Consequences of the Thought

Ask yourself, "If I keep believing this thought, how will it affect me?" If a thought blocks you from trying new things or keeps you stressed every day, it is probably not a thought you want to hold onto. That does not mean you deny the idea of risk, but you may want to shape it in a way that allows more freedom.

Step 12: Gather Facts from the Outside

If you are worried about something specific—like your performance at work—see if you can gather direct feedback instead of guessing. You might ask a colleague or manager for honest input. If you worry your friend is mad at you, consider asking them calmly rather than stewing in assumptions. Facts can calm the mind more than guesswork.

Step 13: Use Small Experiments

Sometimes, you can test an unhelpful thought by running a little experiment. If you believe you cannot talk to strangers without panicking, you might practice a short interaction at a store, just saying a brief hello. Note how it feels. Was it truly impossible, or did you manage, even if you felt nervous? These real-life tests help break the certainty of negative beliefs.

Step 14: Watch for Shifting Standards

Anxious thoughts often shift the goalposts. For example, if you do well on a test, you might then tell yourself, "That test was easy, so it does not count." If you finish a big project, you might say, "Well, it only went okay because I got lucky." This pattern discounts positive evidence and keeps the negative belief alive. Notice if you do this. Challenge it by allowing yourself to accept success when it occurs.

Step 15: Balance the Tone of Your Self-Talk

When fear is high, self-talk can swing to extremes. We might say, "Everything is awful," or "I can't handle anything." Try adding a "but" statement: "I feel overwhelmed, but I have handled tough days before." Or "I am scared now, but I can do one small step." This does not remove the fear, yet it keeps the conversation balanced.

Step 16: Track Your Progress

As you work on challenging thoughts, you might keep a log of specific times you replaced an unhelpful thought with a more balanced one. Mark down how you felt before and after. Over time, you will see patterns of improvement. You may notice that certain times of day or certain triggers bring out the worst thoughts, so you can be ready for them.

Step 17: Linking Thoughts with Values

If a thought says, "I will never be brave enough to speak in public," recall your personal values and goals. Maybe you value personal growth or you care about sharing your ideas at work. By linking your choice to your deeper values, you have a stronger reason to challenge the fear-driven thought. You might say, "I am scared, but I value speaking up for what is right, so I will try anyway." This can give you the push you need to move past the anxiety.

Step 18: Seek Feedback from Supportive People

Combine the methods of this chapter with your support system from Chapter 11. Ask a trusted friend, "I keep thinking I will fail my driving test. Does that sound realistic to you?" Let them share an outside perspective. They might point out evidence of your ability or remind you of similar tasks you handled well. This external view can poke holes in your negative assumptions.

Step 19: Notice Where You Are in the Day

Anxious thoughts can be stronger at certain times—like late at night, when you are tired and less able to think clearly. If you realize your negative ideas come on when you are exhausted, try not to trust them fully at that moment. You might say, "I am too tired to judge this well; I will wait until morning to decide if this worry is valid." Sometimes a good night's rest changes how we see things.

Step 20: Accept Some Uncertainty

We cannot know or control everything. Some anxious thoughts come from the wish to be 100% sure of outcomes. Challenging them may involve admitting that life has unknowns. You might say, "I do not know for certain that things will work out, but I can still choose how to respond right now." This acceptance can lower the pressure to be sure of every detail.

Putting It All Together

Challenging unhelpful thoughts takes practice, patience, and a willingness to question your own mind. Over time, you become quicker at spotting negative thinking patterns and less inclined to believe them outright. This does not mean you stop feeling fear entirely, but it often means you can keep going in spite of it.

When we pair these thought-challenging methods with the daily calming skills, routines, and support networks discussed in earlier chapters, we form a strong approach to reducing anxiety. You might still feel worried before a big event, but you will no longer be stuck in a mental loop that says disaster is certain.

Conclusion of Chapter 12

Challenging unhelpful thoughts is at the core of growing better habits in the fight against **fear** and **anxiety**. By identifying patterns like catastrophic thinking or all-or-nothing beliefs, and by asking yourself to provide real evidence, you begin to see how your mind shapes your stress. Over time, you can guide your thoughts toward a clearer view of reality—one that includes your ability to cope, learn, and move forward.

PART SEVEN: SHAPING A NEW WAY TO THINK

Welcome to **Part Seven** of this book. You have come a long way, exploring the many sides of **fear** and **anxiety**. You have learned to spot triggers, use daily routines, shape your thoughts, and rely on a healthy support network. Now, in this part, we will talk about **shaping a new way to think**. This will involve two chapters:

1. **Chapter 13: The Power of Self-Talk**
2. **Chapter 14: Turning Stress into a Helpful Force**

By digging into these topics, you will see how the voice in your head can guide or mislead you and how stress can become something more helpful than harmful. Both chapters build on what you have learned so far, giving you new angles to reduce the grip of fear. The goal is to grow a lasting mindset that helps you face challenges with steadiness.

CHAPTER 13: THE POWER OF SELF-TALK

Introduction

Each day, we have a stream of thoughts running in our minds. This inner voice, often called **self-talk**, shapes how we see ourselves and the world around us. It can give us courage or it can tear us down. When fear and anxiety take over, our self-talk might become very harsh. It might label us as failures or see only worst-case outcomes. Over time, that kind of negative inner voice can fuel more fear.

But self-talk is not fixed. We can learn to notice it, guide it, and change its tone. This does not mean forcing ourselves to be unrealistically upbeat. It means learning to speak to ourselves in a way that is **true** and also **helpful**. When we build a kinder, more balanced self-talk, our fears have less space to grow.

In this chapter, we will look at the role of self-talk in fear and anxiety, how to spot negative patterns, and how to shape a healthier internal voice. We will explore the difference between empty affirmations and genuine encouragement. We will also discuss ways to handle self-doubt, using patience rather than harshness. By the end, you will have a clearer picture of how the words you choose to say to yourself can keep you anchored in calmer ground.

The Role of Internal Speech

We all carry an internal speech. It forms our immediate reactions to events. For instance, when we drop a glass, we might think, "Oh, I am so clumsy." Or if we get a task done faster than expected, we might say, "That went well. I am proud of myself." These quick remarks can seem minor, but repeated day after day, they lay down a pattern that shapes our view of life.

For people prone to fear or anxiety, internal speech can tilt negative. We might have an automatic habit of criticizing ourselves or imagining that every slip-up means disaster. This mental chatter is not always loud. Sometimes it is a quiet hum in the background. Yet it can influence how much fear we feel.

When our self-talk is full of **negative labels** or **extreme predictions**, it adds fuel to worry. If we keep telling ourselves we are bound to fail, we start to fear even trying. If we say we cannot trust anyone, we start to expect pain whenever we meet new people. Slowly, our world shrinks.

But there is a silver lining: self-talk is something we can notice and adjust. We can learn to pick better words, to question harsh claims, and to encourage ourselves with sincerity. This does not turn us into perfect beings with zero anxiety. It just gives us a more stable platform to stand on when fear arises.

Common Negative Self-Talk Patterns

1. **Labeling**: Using damaging labels for ourselves, like "I am a loser," "I am weak," or "I am useless." These labels become mental shortcuts. Instead of seeing that we made a small mistake, we leap to a label that sums up our entire worth.

2. **Disqualifying the positive**: We ignore or downplay our good moments. If we handle a problem well, we might say, "That was just luck," rather than giving ourselves credit.
3. **Exaggerating failure**: We treat every error as a massive blunder. Spilling coffee becomes "proof" that we cannot do anything right. A small oversight in a project becomes "I should never try this kind of work again."
4. **Demanding perfection**: Our self-talk might say, "I must do this without any mistakes, or I am a failure." This sets an impossible bar. Any slip triggers shame or despair.
5. **Comparing harshly to others**: We might say, "Everyone else is better at this than I am." This overlooks the fact that we rarely know the full story of other people's struggles.
6. **Catastrophic words**: Terms like "always," "never," "disaster," "ruined," can show up in our inner speech. They turn a single event into a final verdict on everything.

These patterns make fear stronger because they paint a negative storyline in our minds. Over time, we might believe these stories without question, even though they are not based on clear facts.

Why We Cling to Negative Self-Talk

It can seem strange that we hold onto habits that make us feel worse. One reason is that negative thinking sometimes feels safer. By criticizing ourselves first, we think we protect ourselves from outside criticism. Or by imagining worst-case outcomes, we think we are bracing ourselves for trouble. However, this approach only adds daily stress.

In some cases, negative self-talk might stem from how we were raised. If we heard a parent or teacher constantly speak to us in a harsh way, we might continue that pattern inside our own head. The mind repeats old scripts unless we step in.

Another factor is that negative self-talk can be a twisted form of motivation. We might think that if we call ourselves lazy, we will push harder. But fear-based motivation rarely leads to healthy growth. It usually results in more anxiety, perfectionism, or burnout.

Replacing Negative Self-Talk with a Balanced Voice

The key to healthier self-talk is **balance**, not blind positivity. We do not want to replace "I am worthless" with "I am the greatest person who ever lived." Such extremes do not solve the root issue. Instead, we aim for statements that acknowledge reality but also support a kind view of ourselves.

Let us consider an example. Suppose you catch yourself thinking, "I am going to fail this exam, and then my whole life will be ruined." A balanced self-talk might be:

- "I am nervous about this exam, but I have studied and can do my best."
- "Even if I do poorly, it does not mean my life is ruined. I will find a way forward."

Notice how this new voice does not ignore the fear. It admits you are nervous. But it also recognizes that one test is not your entire life. It gives room for a range of possible outcomes, not just the worst one.

Empty Affirmations vs. Realistic Encouragement

There is a trend of using **affirmations** like "I am powerful, I am unstoppable, I am perfect as I am." While this might help some people, it can feel hollow if it clashes with what we truly believe about ourselves. Telling ourselves we are perfect can backfire if deep down we are sure we are not.

Realistic encouragement is more grounded. It might say, "I am learning each day and can handle more than I once thought." Or, "I have strengths and weaknesses, but I am making progress." These messages do not promise miracles. They simply affirm that we are capable and growing.

By choosing honest statements that are still positive, we avoid the tension that comes when our mind says, "That is not true at all." Over time, these messages build a more stable self-view.

Self-Talk in Everyday Life

Self-talk is not just about big events. It also shows up in small, daily moments. For instance, when we drop our keys, do we curse ourselves as "an idiot," or do we calmly say, "Oops, let me pick that up and move on"? When a coworker speaks to us with a slight edge, do we assume, "They hate me," or do we think, "They might be having a bad day"?

These small choices add up. As we practice noticing self-talk in ordinary moments, we build a habit of stepping back from negative leaps. We start to see how many times our internal voice runs toward fear and judgment without cause.

The Language of Encouragement

It helps to think of building an **internal coach** instead of an internal critic. A coach can point out mistakes, but it does so to help us improve, not to tear us down. It also notices what we do well, which fuels motivation.

Imagine you have a friend who is about to run a race. Which voice would help them more?

- Critic's voice: "You will probably trip and embarrass yourself. You never practice enough. You are slow."
- Coach's voice: "You have trained for this, and you can give it your best shot. If you stumble, it is okay—you can keep going."

The critic's voice might think it is being "realistic," but it is actually creating more fear. The coach's voice does not promise a guaranteed win. It just focuses on the idea that effort and resilience matter. That is the balance we want.

Handling Self-Doubt

Self-doubt is a strong emotion. It can creep in when we face new tasks or challenges. Our self-talk might say, "Who do you think you are to try this?" or "You are just going to fail and look foolish."

To deal with this, we can remind ourselves that **everyone** experiences doubt at times. We can name it when it appears: "I sense self-doubt telling me I am not good enough." Naming it helps us see it as just a thought, not a fact. Then we can offer a more balanced reply: "This is new, so it is normal to feel uncertain. I can still try and see what happens."

Reframing Mistakes in Self-Talk

Another place where fear can grow is around **mistakes**. If we see every mistake as proof of a bigger flaw, we will be scared to attempt new things. A better approach is to reframe mistakes as part of learning.

Instead of saying, "I messed up, so I am worthless," we can say, "I messed up, so I can see what went wrong and do better next time." This shift removes the harsh finality of labeling ourselves as flawed. It turns mistakes into stepping stones rather than dead ends.

The Effect of Body Posture on Self-Talk

Our bodies and minds are linked. When we slouch, hang our head, or breathe in a shallow way, we might send signals to our mind that we are defeated. This can color our self-talk in a negative tone.

Try a quick experiment: sit or stand with your shoulders back, arms relaxed, and take a slow breath. Notice if this changes the mood of your self-talk. Often, a more open posture can give the mind a sense of possibility or calm. This does not erase real problems, but it can reduce the feeling of being trapped.

Building a Kind Internal Coach

To build a kind internal coach, you can follow a few simple steps:

1. **Notice the critic**. Every time you catch that harsh voice, pause.
2. **Ask what a fair friend would say**. This helps you shift from blame to support.
3. **Use balanced words**. Focus on honest acceptance and room for growth.
4. **Repeat**. Changing your self-talk is not a one-time fix. You need to do this again and again.

Over time, this new voice becomes more natural. You might still hear the critic, but you learn to override it with the coach that believes in your ability to keep going.

Self-Criticism vs. Self-Reflection

You might wonder, "Is not some self-criticism good? Do I not need to push myself?" There is a difference between **self-criticism** and **self-reflection**. Self-criticism is judgmental. It jumps to personal attacks. Self-reflection is honest. It looks at what happened and asks how we can learn.

- Self-criticism: "I cannot believe I forgot to pay that bill. I am so stupid."
- Self-reflection: "I forgot to pay that bill. I need a better system for reminders so this does not happen again."

One is shaming; the other is problem-solving. Self-reflection helps us improve without adding shame-based fear.

Dealing with Deep-Rooted Negative Beliefs

Some negative beliefs run deep. They may have been with us for years, or they might come from painful experiences. A single chapter on self-talk cannot always resolve these deep issues fully. If you sense a very strong core belief like, "I am unlovable," or "I am broken," it may be wise to speak with a therapist or counselor. They can guide you through structured ways to unpack and shift these beliefs over time.

Even so, practicing day-to-day healthy self-talk can chip away at these beliefs bit by bit. It can show you that, in many moments, those old beliefs do not match reality. You can have small wins, positive interactions, or examples of success that contradict the harmful story you have carried.

Self-Talk and Confidence

Confidence is not just about feeling no fear. It is about trusting you can handle what comes, even if fear is present. Self-talk plays a huge role here. If your mind always says, "You cannot handle this," you lose confidence before you begin. If your mind says, "You can try and learn as you go," confidence grows. You start to see challenges as opportunities instead of traps.

Confidence also does not mean you think you are perfect. It means you believe you have enough ability or enough adaptability to give something a fair attempt.

You accept that you will survive mistakes or setbacks. This, in turn, lowers the overall anxiety level because you no longer see every new task as a threat.

When Self-Talk Intersects with Social Interactions

Sometimes, our self-talk is triggered by how we think others see us. If someone glances our way, we might assume, "They are judging me." If a friend cancels a plan, we might think, "They do not really like me." These are quick leaps that may or may not be true.

In such moments, watch the story your mind is telling. Is there clear evidence for these claims? Could there be another reason for the glance or the canceled plan? By questioning these assumptions, we keep fear from blossoming into full anxiety about rejection or ridicule.

Challenging Self-Talk in Real Time

It can be helpful to break down the steps you take when you spot negative self-talk in the middle of the day:

1. **Pause**: Notice a sudden wave of fear, stress, or gloom.
2. **Identify**: Ask, "What thought did I just have?"
3. **Question**: Check if that thought is fair, balanced, or based on facts.
4. **Rephrase**: Replace it with a statement that is still honest but more supportive.
5. **Move on**: Continue your task or activity, carrying the new statement in mind.

You might not catch every negative thought at first. But even a few moments of correction each day can reduce the overall weight of anxiety.

Avoiding "Toxic Positivity"

"Toxic positivity" is when we deny real problems or valid feelings in an effort to be positive. We might say, "Everything is great!" even if we are in real distress. This does not help in the long run because it ignores reality.

Healthy self-talk allows for sadness, stress, or fear, but it does not blow them out of proportion. It says, "Yes, I am upset right now, and that is valid. I will find ways to cope or seek help." This approach balances honesty with self-kindness.

Stepping Away from Social Comparisons

Sometimes, negative self-talk grows from comparing ourselves with others, especially online. We see curated images of success or happiness and think, "I do not match up." Then our inner voice calls us failures or dull. If you notice this pattern, it might help to set limits on how much you engage in these comparisons. Remind yourself that no one's real life is as flawless as their curated posts.

When self-talk says, "Look at how much better they are," counter with, "They have their own struggles I do not see, and I have my own strengths." This does not create false superiority. It simply acknowledges reality.

Self-Talk During Tough Transitions

Big changes like moving, starting a new job, or ending a relationship can stir up a flood of negative thoughts. We might doubt our choices, fear the unknown, or grieve the loss of what was familiar. In these times, self-talk becomes crucial.

We can remind ourselves that transitions are naturally unsettling. We can say, "I feel uncertain, but that does not mean I made the wrong choice." Or, "It is normal to miss my old routine, but I can adapt to this new place over time." Such statements do not remove the stress of change. They just keep it from spiraling into paralyzing fear.

The Process of Building New Mental Pathways

Every time we challenge negative self-talk, we are shaping new mental pathways in our brain. At first, the old path of negativity feels stronger and more automatic. But as we persist in noticing and rephrasing, the new path gains strength. We start to respond with calmer or kinder thoughts more quickly.

This is similar to learning a new skill, like playing a musical instrument. Early on, we have to consciously force our fingers into the right positions. Over time, it becomes more natural. The same is true for self-talk. What feels awkward at first can become second nature if we keep practicing.

Combining Self-Talk with Other Coping Skills

Self-talk is not the only method. It blends well with the grounding techniques, breathing exercises, and daily routines you have learned in earlier parts of this book. For instance, if you feel a rush of panic, you might pause to breathe slowly, ground yourself by looking at your surroundings, and then speak a calming statement to yourself.

This synergy helps break the chain that leads from small worries to big fears. When your mind tries to pull you into anxiety, you can use self-talk plus a physical relaxation trick. The more tools you combine, the more control you gain over your own reactions.

Moving Toward a Consistent Inner Ally

Ultimately, you want to become your own ally. That does not mean you ignore faults or gloss over real concerns. It means you have a steady friend-like voice inside that can point out issues without shaming, and can praise progress without exaggerating. It stands by you when fear appears, saying, "Yes, this is scary, but you have handled things before and can handle this too."

Such an inner ally can make a huge difference in how you navigate life's ups and downs. It gives you a sense of security that no external crisis can fully remove, because it is rooted in your own way of thinking.

Conclusion of Chapter 13

Self-talk is a powerful factor in managing **fear** and **anxiety**. Negative patterns can fuel our worst worries, while balanced, supportive words can help us see challenges as parts of life that we can face. We build a calmer outlook by noticing harsh or distorted self-talk, questioning it, and practicing a more realistic tone. Over time, this new way of talking to ourselves becomes a core habit that lowers stress.

CHAPTER 14: TURNING STRESS INTO A HELPFUL FORCE

Introduction

Stress is often viewed as the enemy. We blame it for sleepless nights, tense muscles, and jumpy nerves. But what if stress could sometimes be helpful? What if certain kinds of stress can sharpen our focus, encourage us to learn, and make us more capable in the long run?

In this chapter, we will talk about stress in a new way. We will explore the difference between harmful stress (sometimes called "distress") and stress that helps us rise to challenges ("eustress"). We will see how reframing stress can reduce fear and build confidence. We will also look at practical steps to handle stress so that it does not become overwhelming.

Understanding the Stress Response

At the core, stress is the body's response to demands. When we face a threat or a deadline, our brain signals the release of stress hormones like cortisol and adrenaline. Our heart rate goes up, our breathing may quicken, and our senses turn more alert.

In genuine emergencies, this response is useful. It helps us run, fight, or make quick choices. The trouble appears when this reaction is triggered too often or too strongly. Then we experience chronic stress, which can harm our physical and mental health.

Still, not all stress is the same. There is a kind of stress that can spark growth if we handle it wisely.

Eustress vs. Distress

- **Distress** is the stress we usually think of: it feels uncomfortable, draining, and scary. It comes from demands we view as beyond our capacity or from threats that seem too big to handle.

- **Eustress** is a positive, motivating kind of stress. It might show up when we tackle a project we care about, compete in a sport, or learn a challenging new skill. We feel the rush of challenge, but we also feel able to handle it.

The same event can be distress or eustress depending on how we view it. For instance, a public speech might be distress if we tell ourselves, "I cannot do this, and everyone will judge me." It might be eustress if we say, "This is a big moment, but I am excited to share my ideas."

Reframing Stress as a Sign of Readiness

One way to turn stress into something helpful is to see it as a **sign** that we are active and engaged. If we never felt stress, we might never push ourselves out of comfort zones. A mild level of stress can keep us alert, help us focus, and push us to prepare carefully.

Instead of saying, "I am stressed, so this is bad," we can say, "I feel stress, which means I care about this. My body is gearing up to do its best." This shift in perspective can ease the fear that stress means failure.

Balancing Challenge and Skills

There is a concept called "flow," which happens when our skills match the challenge at hand. If the task is too easy, we get bored; if it is too hard, we get anxious. But if it is challenging enough to keep us interested, yet within reach of our abilities, we enter a state of deep focus.

Eustress often appears in this "flow zone." We feel stretched, but not shattered. We might lose track of time because we are fully immersed. This is a healthy form of stress that drives growth.

Setting Realistic Challenges

If we want to tap into eustress, we can pick challenges that are a bit beyond our comfort but not so far that they become overwhelming. For example, if you are new to running, aiming for a short jog each day might be a good stress that promotes health. Trying to run a full marathon next week, without training, might be distress that leads to injury or burnout.

By setting realistic challenges, we give ourselves a chance to succeed in steps. Each success boosts confidence and lowers the fear of future tasks.

The Mind-Body Link in Stress

Stress impacts the body, but the way we think about stress also affects how the body responds. Studies have shown that when people view stress as harmful, their bodies show more harmful stress markers. When they view stress as a sign of readiness, those markers can be less damaging.

This does not mean we should deny stress or ignore it. It means a shift in mindset—seeing stress as part of being alive and active—can lower the negative impact. We still need rest and recovery, but we do not have to fear every uptick in heart rate as a sign of doom.

Daily Routines to Channel Stress

Stress is easier to manage if we have routines that include both effort and recovery. This might look like:

- A set work schedule with short breaks to unwind.
- Regular exercise that challenges us, followed by proper rest.
- Time to socialize or engage in hobbies that help us recharge.

When we treat ourselves like athletes preparing for a series of games, we recognize the need for cycles of activity and rest. This can channel stress into performance when needed, but also prevent overload.

Rest as a Key Part of Growth

Rest is not laziness. It is the time when the body and mind repair themselves, sorting out the experiences we have had. If we push ourselves without rest, stress becomes chronic and harmful. If we balance effort with recovery, we can handle higher levels of stress over time.

That is why good sleep, proper nutrition, and moments of pause during the day are essential. They set the stage for stress to become eustress rather than distress.

Celebrating Small Wins

One reason stress feels discouraging is that we forget to celebrate the progress we make. If we only notice big achievements, we miss the daily steps that lead us there. Recognizing small wins can help us see stress as worthwhile.

For example, if your goal is to speak confidently in group settings, a small win might be sharing one comment in a meeting. That might cause stress, but once you do it, you can say, "I took a step forward." This feeling of small victory can motivate you to keep facing the stress of speaking until it becomes easier.

The Fear-Stress Connection

Fear often grows when we see stress as an enemy. We might think, "I feel stressed, so this must be dangerous." Or, "Stress means I am not coping well." In reality, some stress is normal in many situations that matter—job interviews, first dates, important tests. By learning to accept that stress can be part of doing something valuable, we reduce the fear that it is a sign of failure.

Turning Anxiety into Readiness

Sometimes we can rename anxiety as **readiness**. Instead of saying, "I am anxious about this upcoming race," we can say, "I feel excited energy because I am about to do something challenging." The physical signs—faster heartbeat, quickening breath—can be similar in both anxiety and excitement. The main difference is the story we attach to them.

Of course, if the stress is too intense or lasts too long, it can still be harmful. But in many day-to-day cases, labeling that nervous energy as readiness can keep fear from exploding into panic.

Handling Social Stress

Social situations often create stress, especially if we fear judgment or rejection. But those settings can also be chances for **connection**, **growth**, or **learning** new skills (like public speaking). If we see every social event as a threat, we lock ourselves into avoidance. If we see it as a challenge that might bring good outcomes, we open a door to eustress.

One practical way is to set a small social goal, like talking to two new people at a gathering. It might feel stressful, but achieving it can give a burst of confidence. Over time, you might find you no longer see such events as purely scary because you have turned them into small challenges you can handle.

Stress as a Teacher

Stressful moments can teach us about our limits, priorities, and passions. If something stresses us a lot, it might indicate we care deeply about it. If we feel no stress, maybe it does not matter much to us. By paying attention to how stress moves in our life, we can learn about ourselves.

We might also learn what triggers unhelpful levels of stress. For instance, if last-minute deadlines always push you over the edge, you can plan to start tasks earlier. If certain conflicts at work raise your stress to distress levels, you can seek conflict-resolution strategies. Stress alerts us to changes we may need to make.

The Role of Goals and Purpose

Having a **sense of purpose** can transform how we handle stress. If we know why we are facing a challenge, stress feels more tolerable. We see it as part of a meaningful effort rather than pointless pain. This does not remove all discomfort, but it can give us the mental energy to endure.

For example, a student might find exams stressful, but if they connect it to the goal of learning a skill that matters for their future, it becomes eustress. A worker might see an upcoming presentation as a path to share ideas that could help the company. By focusing on the bigger purpose, we reduce fear and harness stress in a positive way.

Flow and Performance

Earlier, we mentioned "flow," which is a state of complete involvement in a task that challenges you just enough. Stress can push us into flow if we match the difficulty of the task with our current skill. In this state, time can pass quickly and we might even enjoy the sense of focus and progress. This shows how stress, in the right amount, can lead to peak performance, not just panic.

Protecting Against Burnout

Even good stress can become bad if we do not pace ourselves. Burnout occurs when we overload ourselves with too many challenges without enough rest or emotional support. Signs of burnout might include constant exhaustion, loss of interest in what once motivated us, or feeling numb.

To avoid burnout, keep an eye on your schedule and your emotional well-being. If you notice you are constantly drained, reduce some demands or ask for help. A short break, a change of pace, or a lighter workload for a while might be what you need to bounce back.

Learning to Say "No" When Needed

Part of turning stress into a helpful force is knowing when to say "no." Not every challenge is worth taking on. If your plate is already full, adding more demands can push you from eustress into distress. Balancing your responsibilities means allowing yourself the option to decline tasks that do not match your priorities.

This can be tough if you worry about disappointing others. But in the long run, saying "no" when you must can protect your well-being and let you focus on the stress that aligns with your goals.

Stress and Personal Growth

We often grow the most in times of stress that we manage well. Think of athletes training hard to improve performance or artists pushing through creative blocks. The process can be intense, but it leads to new levels of skill. Once we have faced a certain level of stress and conquered it, our baseline for fear can shift. We realize we can handle more than we thought, which reduces future anxiety.

Practical Steps to Reframe Stress

1. **Identify the source**: Ask yourself where this stress is coming from. Is it a big project, a social event, or a life change?
2. **Question your view**: Are you labeling it as a threat or a chance to grow? Could you see it as a puzzle to solve?
3. **Plan for success**: Break the task into smaller parts. Prepare as needed so you feel more capable.

4. **Use a supportive mindset**: Talk to yourself with encouragement: "I can do one step at a time."
5. **Seek help if needed**: Talk with friends or a professional if stress feels too big to handle alone.
6. **Celebrate progress**: Acknowledge each small victory.

Anxiety vs. Readiness

It is helpful to notice the difference between pure anxiety and a readiness for action. Anxiety can feel like dread. Readiness can feel like alertness. Both can raise your heart rate, but the mindset differs. If you start to say, "I am dreading this," try to shift toward, "I am keyed up for this." This small change can redirect fear into focused effort.

Changing the Body's Reaction

In moments of stress, a few physical adjustments can help. A brief round of slow breathing can calm racing thoughts. Loosening tight shoulders or unclenching your jaw can signal your body that you are not in mortal danger, just facing a challenge. Taking breaks to move around or stretch can prevent the build-up of tension.

Using Stress to Build Resilience

Each time we successfully navigate stress, we become more **resilient**. Resilience is not about never feeling pressure. It is about bouncing back from it faster, learning from it, and continuing on with more skill than before.

Over time, you might look back at situations that once scared you and realize they now feel routine. That is because you have grown. What was once distress can become manageable or even exciting. This natural progress is one of the rewards of facing stress head-on rather than fleeing it.

Conclusion of Chapter 14

Stress can be more than a burden if we see it in a balanced way. It can drive us to learn, adapt, and move forward. By recognizing the difference between **eustress** and **distress**, we open the door to using stress as a helpful force rather than letting it paralyze us with fear. This is not about avoiding rest or ignoring real limits. It is about understanding that some stress is part of living a full and purposeful life.

You have now finished **Part Seven**, which focused on **shaping a new way to think**. Chapter 13 showed how **self-talk** can become either a barrier or a support, and Chapter 14 demonstrated how **stress** might be turned into a tool for growth. In the next part—**Part Eight**—we will move toward the topic of **social and group settings**, exploring how fear appears in public spaces and how to keep a better balance between work and personal life. By blending the mindset shifts of Part Seven with the concrete skills from earlier chapters, you will be better prepared to meet the outside world without letting fear call the shots.

PART EIGHT: SOCIAL AND GROUP SETTINGS

You have worked through many parts of this book, gaining insights on **fear** and **anxiety**, finding daily tools, shaping a more balanced mindset, and learning to handle stress in a calmer way. Now, in **Part Eight**, we will look at **social and group settings**. These are the places where fear often shows up in strong ways, whether it is speaking in public, going to crowded gatherings, or juggling all the roles we play in life.

This part has two chapters:

- Chapter 15: Facing Fear in Public Spaces
- Chapter 16: Keeping Balance Between Work and Personal Life

By exploring these topics, you will gain ideas on how to step into public areas with more steadiness and how to avoid letting stress from one part of life spill over into another. This is about forming healthy social connections and routines that keep fear in check, rather than letting it rule your choices in group settings.

CHAPTER 15: FACING FEAR IN PUBLIC SPACES

Introduction

Stepping into public spaces can bring up strong **fear** or **anxiety**. This might show up as sweaty palms, racing thoughts, or a sudden wish to run. Some people feel uneasy in crowded areas, while others worry about speaking up in a meeting or at a social event. In all these cases, the presence of many people or the sense of being watched can trigger fear.

In this chapter, we will talk about why public settings can spark fear, how it might feel, and what steps you can take to stay calmer. We will also look at strategies for different kinds of public challenges: crowded events, group discussions, or even performing on stage. By the end, you should have a clearer roadmap for handling public fear without letting it push you away from places or activities you want to join.

Why Public Settings Can Trigger Fear

There are many reasons why being in a group or public area can bring up anxious feelings. One major cause is the sense that people may judge us. We might worry about how we look, what we say, or how we act. We might fear that others will see our flaws or laugh at our mistakes.

Another cause is the loss of control. In big crowds, we cannot control who bumps into us, who might speak to us, or how the event will flow. This uncertainty can spark fear. We might ask, "What if something goes wrong? Where do I escape? Will I find my way out?"

Some people also have past experiences that increase public fear. Maybe they had a bad moment in front of a group, and now they carry that memory like a warning sign. Or perhaps they grew up hearing that the outside world is dangerous. These messages can linger, shaping how they feel in public places.

Recognizing the Signs of Public Anxiety

When we step into a public space and fear sets in, the body and mind often react in noticeable ways. We might feel tense in our shoulders, notice a racing heart, or sense our breath becoming short. Our mind might speed up with thoughts like, "What if I cannot handle this?" or "Everyone is staring at me."

These feelings can build into a loop. The more we notice our body reacting, the more we think something is wrong, which adds more stress. If we do not step in with coping tools, this can grow into panic, causing us to flee or freeze.

Starting Small: Approaching Crowded Places with Care

If big crowds make you uneasy, it can help to start with smaller steps. You might visit a less-crowded store at a quiet time of day, focusing on keeping your breath steady and reminding yourself that you are safe. Over time, you can pick slightly busier settings, building your comfort level bit by bit.

While this gradual approach takes patience, it can reshape how your body and mind react to crowds. Each small success sends a message that says, "We got through that. It was not as bad as we feared." With repetition, the dread of crowds can ease.

Techniques for Group Discussions or Meetings

Many people struggle with fear when they must speak in a group, whether it is at work, in a class, or among friends. This might come from the thought, "What if I sound foolish?" or "Everyone is paying attention to me." To handle this, you can prepare in a few ways:

- Plan one or two points you want to share. You do not need a full speech, just a short statement to give structure.
- Practice a calming step right before you speak—maybe a single slow breath or a quick reminder: "I do not have to be perfect. I can just share my idea."
- After you speak, notice what actually happened. Did people laugh at you? Or did they simply listen and move on? Often, we see that our biggest fears did not come true.

The more you engage in group talks, the more natural it can become. You might still feel a bit nervous, but it will no longer stop you from sharing your thoughts.

Managing Performance Fears

Some people face fear when they must perform—giving a presentation, singing, or showing their skills in public. Performance fear is common. Even experienced performers often feel nervous. The goal is not to eliminate nerves, but to keep them at a level that does not derail you.

One approach is to practice relaxation before going on stage or into the spotlight. This might include a short breathing exercise, a moment of silent focus, or thinking of a supportive phrase like, "I am ready to do my best." If your heart races, remind yourself that extra energy can help you be more alert and expressive. Try to see the nerves as a sign that you care about doing well, not as proof you will fail.

Setting Boundaries in Public

Sometimes, public fear grows because we do not feel safe setting limits. Maybe we fear saying "no" when people invade our space, or we feel we must always go along with group plans. Learning to set a boundary can reduce anxiety. For instance, if you need a break during a crowded event, you can find a quieter corner for a short time. If someone pressures you to stay longer than you want, you can politely say you have other things to do or that you need some fresh air.

These small steps show your mind that you have some control over the situation. You are not stuck. Even in a busy setting, you can make choices that respect your comfort level.

Using Anchors to Ground Yourself

When you feel overwhelmed in a public place, it helps to have an "anchor" that keeps you from spiraling. An anchor can be something physical, like a small object in your pocket, or a mental image. Some people pick a soothing phrase to repeat, such as, "I am safe right now," or "I can do small steps."

If your thoughts start racing about how many people are around, gently shift to focusing on your anchor. Remind yourself you can handle the moment. Over time, this practice can teach your mind to stay more stable amid the noise.

Re-thinking the Spotlight Effect

Often in public, we feel like everyone is watching us. This is called the "spotlight effect." In truth, most people are busy with their own lives and might not notice every detail about you. Reminding yourself of this can lessen the fear that every slip will be seen and judged.

You could say, "People are probably focused on their own concerns. They might glance at me, but they are not analyzing my every move." By lowering the sense that all eyes are on you, you reduce the intensity of public fear.

Avoiding Complete Avoidance

When fear gets strong, we might dodge public spaces entirely or refuse to speak in groups. While this can bring short-term relief, it tends to make fear stronger in the long run. We never learn that we can survive or even succeed in public. Over time, our world can shrink, which can lead to isolation or missed chances.

It is better to take slow, planned steps to face public settings. Start with easier situations, use your coping skills, and give yourself credit for each step. If you slip up or get overwhelmed, do not see it as a total failure. Learn from it, rest, and try again in a smaller way. Persistence over time can pay off.

Handling Negative Thoughts Mid-Social Event

Even if we plan ahead, negative ideas can pop up in the middle of a social gathering. We might think, "I am so awkward," or "They must think I am weird." When this happens, try a quick mental check: "Is there clear proof that I am awkward, or is this fear talking?" If there is no proof, label it as a worry rather than a fact.

You can also give yourself a small break—go to the restroom or step outside for a minute. Take a few slow breaths, let the tension drop, and then return. This short pause can keep negative thoughts from taking over.

Finding Support in Public Situations

It can help to share your worries with a friend or ally who understands. If you are going to a large event, you might have a signal with that person when you need a break, or you could agree to chat privately for a moment if the noise gets too intense. Knowing you have someone on your side can cut anxiety in half.

If you do not have a friend around, you can still find small ways to feel less alone. Sometimes, chatting briefly with a stranger can ground you. A friendly "hello" or comment on the event can remind you that others are not all hostile or judging. Small bits of connection often reduce the sense of being on the outside.

Checking for Physical Needs

Public fear can worsen if you are already under physical strain. Maybe you are hungry, thirsty, or tired. Addressing these needs can keep your stress response from flaring too fast. Having a snack, sipping water, or finding a seat can all lower tension. This might sound basic, but it often gets overlooked when fear is swirling.

Handling Group Pressure

In some groups, there can be subtle pressure to act a certain way or follow the crowd. If fear makes us too eager to please, we may say yes to things that are not good for us. Over time, this builds resentment or makes us dread being in the group.

Part of facing public fear is learning how to assert yourself. You can practice small statements like, "I am not comfortable with that," or "I will sit this round out." This might feel scary at first, but it can protect you from bigger stress later. It also shows the group where your boundaries are, which can earn respect in the long run.

When Professional Help May Be Useful

If public fear is so strong that you cannot function in daily life, it may be time to seek counseling or therapy. Professionals can teach specialized methods, such as exposure therapy or social skills training, to help you face social settings more gradually. They can also help you uncover any deeper reasons behind your fear, giving you a more solid base to stand on.

There is no shame in seeking help. Many people find that even a few sessions with a mental health worker can shift their perspective and give them new coping tools.

Reflecting on Small Successes

Whenever you face a public setting, take a moment afterward to note any small victory. Maybe you walked through a busy market without leaving early, or you spoke up in a meeting even though your voice trembled a bit. Each time, you show yourself you can handle more than you once believed.

Do not wait for "perfect" performances to feel proud. Fear thrives on ignoring our good steps. By pausing to see them, we balance the mind's tendency to highlight mistakes.

Conclusion of Chapter 15

Facing **fear** in public spaces can be challenging, but it does not have to rule your life. By starting small, using grounding methods, and reminding yourself that you deserve to take up space in the world, you can slowly tame the anxiety that appears in group settings. This is not about becoming fearless overnight. It is about building enough trust in your own skills and coping methods so that public places, events, and conversations do not feel off-limits.

In **Chapter 16**, we will look at how to keep **balance** between work and personal life. Many of us juggle tasks and roles in a hectic way, and that stress can leak into social settings or feed our anxieties. By learning to set clear boundaries and manage our time wisely, we can protect our mental and emotional health. Blending these strategies with what you have learned about facing public fear will give you a better grasp on how to shape a steady life in all environments.

CHAPTER 16: KEEPING BALANCE BETWEEN WORK AND PERSONAL LIFE

Introduction

Modern life often demands that we keep multiple roles: worker, student, parent, partner, friend, volunteer, and more. We might dash from one task to the next, leaving little room for rest. This constant rush can spark or feed **fear** and **anxiety**, making our minds feel overloaded.

In this chapter, we will talk about how to find **balance** between work responsibilities and personal life. We will see how too much pressure in one area can spill over into the other, creating a cycle of stress. We will also look at ways to set boundaries, manage time, and preserve our emotional energy. By doing this, we lower the risk that fear takes root in every corner of our day.

Recognizing the Signs of Imbalance

A lack of balance often shows up in small but telling ways:

- You feel constantly rushed or behind schedule.
- You skip meals or do not sleep enough because of work demands.
- You cannot enjoy time with loved ones because you keep thinking about work tasks.
- You feel guilty when resting, as though you should be working.
- You have no energy for hobbies or personal interests that once brought joy.

These signs might seem normal in a fast-paced world, but they can signal that your life load is leaning too far in one direction. Over time, this imbalance can feed anxiety, as your mind senses you never fully relax or re-energize.

The Impact on Fear and Anxiety

When our minds are stretched thin by too many duties, fear can grow. We worry about dropping the ball or failing to meet expectations. We might lie awake, dreading the next day's tasks, or we might struggle to focus because of mental fatigue.

We can also become irritable, making conflicts at work or home more likely. This adds to stress, further fueling anxiety. Without action, this cycle can spin out of control, leaving us feeling trapped. Yet we do have choices to shape our schedule and protect our health.

Setting Clear Work Boundaries

One key step is to decide when work begins and ends. If we let work seep into all hours—checking emails in bed, answering calls during family time—our mind never fully switches off. Over time, this can lead to burnout.

Try to create a firm boundary around work time. If possible, set a cutoff hour in the evening when you stop responding to work messages. Let coworkers or clients know that you will reply the next morning. This might be tricky at first, but it is vital for mental rest.

Communicating Your Limits

Sometimes, we fear telling our boss, teammates, or friends that we cannot take on more tasks. We might worry they will see us as lazy or weak. But constantly saying yes to extra work or demands can leave us drained.

Learning to say "I do not have the bandwidth for that right now" is a skill that reduces long-term anxiety. If you explain your current obligations calmly, many people will understand. If they do not, that is a sign the environment might not be supportive of healthy balance.

Planning the Day with Realistic Goals

Too often, we fill our to-do lists with more tasks than we can handle. This sets us up for stress. A better way is to list the most important tasks first, ensuring that those get your main energy. Then, if time allows, you can address smaller or less urgent tasks.

If you realize partway through the day that you cannot finish everything, you can reorganize. Pushing yourself to do it all at any cost usually leads to rushed or poor results, plus more anxiety. Consistent, realistic daily planning leaves room for breaks and keeps your workload manageable.

Creating Personal Time Blocks

To keep balance, plan personal activities as well. These are times for rest, hobbies, or social life. If we do not schedule them, work or other duties might fill every gap. Mark these blocks on your calendar if that helps you treat them seriously.

Personal time could be a short walk, reading a bit each morning, cooking a meal in peace, or meeting a friend for coffee. The point is to carve out moments that remind you life is not just about tasks. Over time, these pauses can recharge your mental batteries.

Handling Work-From-Home Challenges

Working from home can blur the line between job and personal life even more. It is easy to stay "on" all day, never stepping away from the computer. If you face this, set up a separate work area if possible. Change clothes after work hours to signal your mind it is time to relax. Resist the urge to check emails late at night. Treat your home office as if it were a traditional workplace in terms of start and stop times.

Dealing with Guilt over Rest

Many people feel guilty when they rest, as though they are wasting time. But rest is not wasted time; it is fuel. Just like a car cannot run without gas, your mind and body cannot function well without breaks. Remind yourself that rest is part of being productive in a sustainable way.

If guilt appears, note it as a thought: "I notice I am feeling guilty about relaxing." Then question it: "Is it truly wrong to take a break, or am I pushing an unrealistic ideal?" Often, you will see that the guilt does not match reality. You need rest to do your best.

Boundaries with Technology

Smartphones and laptops can keep us tethered to work or social media all day. This constant connection can raise anxiety, as we never fully disconnect. Consider turning off notifications for certain apps during personal hours. You might also store work devices in a different room after a set time.

If you find yourself scrolling late at night, ask if this is helping or if it is fueling stress. Sometimes, setting a no-screen rule 30 minutes before bed can improve sleep, which in turn lowers daily anxiety.

Family and Relationship Communication

Balancing work and personal life is not just about your own schedule. If you live with others, talk about what you need. Maybe you need one night a week to recharge alone. Maybe you need help with chores so you are not overburdened. Communicating calmly can prevent misunderstandings and lower tension.

If family members feel you are too distracted by work, you can agree on specific times to give them your full attention. This is not about ignoring your duties but finding an arrangement that respects everyone's needs.

Juggling Multiple Roles

Some people have many roles: employee, parent, caregiver, student, and more. It can help to think of each role as a hat you put on at certain times. When you are wearing the "parent hat," focus on that. When you switch to the "work hat," let yourself commit to work tasks. This mental shift can reduce confusion, keeping you present in whichever role you are playing at that moment.

Of course, emergencies arise when roles overlap, like a sick child during a busy workday. But if day-to-day life has clear time blocks for each role, the overlap is less chaotic, lowering the general sense of stress.

Taking Stock of Your Commitments

Sometimes, we take on more than we truly want or need. This could be extra volunteer roles, social obligations, or side projects. While these can be good, if they pile up, they can leave no space for rest. Take a moment to list all your commitments and ask: "Do I really need to do all of these?" If not, consider stepping back from some.

People often fear disappointing others, but if you constantly run on empty, you might not serve anyone well. By dropping a few optional tasks, you free up energy to do better at the core duties and keep a calmer mind.

Strategies for High-Pressure Work Environments

If your workplace is truly high-pressure, with constant deadlines or demands, you might need extra steps. This could include learning short relaxation methods you can do at your desk, like a quick breath exercise. Or negotiating with your manager about realistic workloads. If stress is severe, consider whether a different job or department might be healthier for you.

While we cannot always change a workplace overnight, small steps—like sharing concerns with a colleague or finding a mentor—can ease the weight. You might also form or join a support group of coworkers who share tips on handling work stress.

Mental Breaks During the Day

Even on busy days, short mental breaks can restore balance. A minute of slow breathing, a short walk, or even closing your eyes to gather your thoughts can lower tension. Set an alarm if needed, reminding yourself to pause every few hours. This might feel strange at first, but it can stop you from drifting into continuous stress mode.

Learning to Pace Yourself Over the Week

Not every day has to be jam-packed. If you have control over your schedule, spread out demanding tasks so you are not overwhelmed on a single day. Some days might still be busier than others, but aim to keep at least one or two lighter days in the week for errands, rest, or social time. This helps prevent the buildup of fear about an endless cycle of tasks.

Vacation and Time Off

If possible, take regular days off or occasional vacations. Plan them in a way that truly separates you from work or other draining duties. This might mean turning on an out-of-office message or even leaving your phone behind for a day trip. The point is to experience a real mental reset. These breaks can lower long-term anxiety and restore energy for the tasks ahead.

Recognizing Personal Warning Signs

Everyone has unique signals that they are losing balance. For some, it might be insomnia. For others, it might be a short fuse or a sense of constant worry. Learning your own warning signs helps you step back and adjust your routine before bigger problems arise.

If you realize you have been snapping at loved ones or feeling panic over small tasks, pause. Look at your schedule. Are you overcommitting? Are you letting work eat into rest times? By catching these patterns early, you can save yourself from deeper anxiety down the line.

Seeking Help for Chronic Imbalance

If you find it impossible to create balance, it may be time to speak with a counselor or life coach. Sometimes, we have deep beliefs or patterns that make us say "yes" to everything or take on too much. Professional guidance can help you untangle these roots and set a plan for healthier limits.

In some cases, couples or family counseling can help if your home life is a big source of stress. When everyone in the household learns to communicate needs and share tasks, it can ease the load on one person.

Linking Work-Life Balance to Overall Health

Chronic imbalance can harm more than your mental state. It can lead to physical health issues like headaches, high blood pressure, or digestion problems. By keeping a steadier balance, you care for your whole self. You also show people around you that a healthy life includes space for both duty and rest.

Stepping Toward a Balanced Mindset

Building a work-life balance is not a one-time fix. It is a mindset shift. You begin to see that you are not a machine. You have needs for rest, growth, and enjoyment outside of your duties. When you honor these needs, fear and anxiety often drop because you feel more complete. You are not defined only by your output, but by your well-being too.

Conclusion of Chapter 16

Keeping **balance** between work and personal life can protect us from **fear** and **anxiety** growing out of control. By setting boundaries, planning realistic tasks, and allowing time for rest and personal interests, we form a lifestyle that supports mental stability. This does not mean life will always be easy. But it does mean we can avoid the trap of constant overload.

Part Eight has guided you through **social and group settings** and the importance of **work-life balance**. In Chapter 15, we looked at how to handle public fear by using steady steps and coping methods. Now, in Chapter 16, we have explored how to keep your roles and duties in check so that fear does not rise from an endless cycle of demands. In **Part Nine**, we will explore how to **stay steady** when setbacks appear and how to make purposeful changes in your routine. The progress you have made so far sets the groundwork for these next chapters, where you will learn to cope with obstacles in a flexible, confident way.

PART NINE: STAYING STEADY

You have come a long way in learning about **fear** and **anxiety**, spotting triggers, using routines, reshaping negative thoughts, and handling public settings. Now, in **Part Nine**, we will focus on **staying steady**, even when things go wrong. This part has two chapters:

- Chapter 17: Coping with Setbacks and Slips
- Chapter 18: Making Purposeful Changes

These chapters will help you face the times when fear comes back or when you stumble on your path. They will show how you can make corrections without giving up on the progress you have already made. By the end, you will see that setbacks do not mean you have failed. They are just part of being human. You can learn to handle slips in a calmer way and keep moving toward a life where fear does not rule your choices.

CHAPTER 17: COPING WITH SETBACKS AND SLIPS

Introduction

No matter how much you learn or practice, you will have tough days. Fear or anxiety might come rushing back when you least expect it. You might find yourself avoiding a social event after weeks of steady progress, or you might have an outburst at work that you thought you had moved beyond. These **setbacks and slips** can feel discouraging. You might think all your effort was wasted.

But setbacks and slips are not signs of failure. They are part of normal growth. When we try to change habits, we rarely move in a straight line. Sometimes, we find ourselves back in old patterns, but with new skills and awareness. In this chapter, we will explore why setbacks happen, how to handle them with less fear, and how to use them as learning tools. You will see that even if the path is not smooth, you can still keep going with a sense of purpose.

Why Setbacks Appear

Fear and anxiety habits can run deep. They might be tied to childhood memories, strong beliefs about the world, or physical reactions we have carried for years. Even after some progress, triggers can show up that catch us off guard. We might face a new situation that feels overwhelming, or we might be under more stress than usual.

Life events can also spark old fears. A new job, a loss, an illness, or a sudden change can cause us to slip into protective behaviors we once used. We might not even realize we are doing it until we feel that familiar wave of panic or dread.

It is natural to hope that once we learn coping methods, fear will never return. But that is not how the mind works. We can reduce the power of fear, but we cannot erase it entirely. Sometimes, a slip is just the mind's way of saying, "I am under stress, and I am going back to what I know." Our goal is to spot that quicker and bring ourselves back to balance sooner.

Spotting the Early Signs of a Slip

A slip often starts with small signals. We might skip our usual calming routine for a few days or notice we are avoiding calls from friends. We might find ourselves snapping at small things or having trouble sleeping because worries are spinning again. These clues might seem minor, but they can hint that old fear patterns are creeping back.

If we catch these signs early, we have a better chance to correct course. We can remind ourselves to use the tools we have learned—slow breathing, grounding, or realistic self-talk. We can reach out to someone in our support network rather than waiting until the fear grows. Early action can stop a small wobble from turning into a full spiral.

Accepting the Reality of Setbacks

One big step is to **accept** that setbacks can happen. This does not mean you want them, but you stop treating them as proof you are failing. Instead, you see them as part of the process. This mindset shift lowers the shame or panic that can come with a slip.

When you accept that fear might return, you stop blaming yourself so harshly. You do not say, "I cannot believe I messed up again. I am hopeless." You say, "I hit a rough patch. That is hard, but I can use my tools to handle it." This kind of view can keep you from piling on extra stress or giving up.

Self-Compassion During a Slip

When setbacks happen, self-talk can become nasty. We might call ourselves weak or foolish. Yet in these moments, **self-compassion** is more important than ever. A kind thought could be, "I feel scared right now. That is not a crime. I can still move forward step by step."

You can also look at what you would say to a friend who had a slip. You would likely be understanding, not cruel. Treating yourself the same way can ease the sting of setbacks. This is not about letting yourself off the hook if you need to make changes, but it is about stopping needless self-punishment.

Using Setbacks as Clues

A slip can reveal areas where you need more practice or support. For instance, if you notice that you panic when plans change at the last minute, you might think, "This is a clue that I struggle with unpredictability. I can focus on ways to handle sudden changes better."

Instead of seeing a setback as a random failure, see it as a clue. Ask, "What triggered this slip? Was I overtired, under stress, or feeling unwell? Did something happen that reminded me of an old fear?" By answering these questions, you gain insight that helps you strengthen your coping methods.

Adjusting Your Strategies

If a slip happens, it might mean your existing strategies need a tweak. For example, if you have been relying on grounding exercises but they are losing their effect, you might try a new approach or combine grounding with another tool like safe imagery or gentle movement.

Sometimes, we get bored with the same routine or we skip steps because we feel better. Then fear reappears. In that case, we might return to a daily practice of slow breathing or mindful breaks, even if we thought we did not need them anymore. The idea is to adjust rather than abandon your progress.

Talking It Out with Your Support System

A slip can feel lonely, especially if you think everyone else is moving forward without issues. Talking with a friend, family member, or counselor can help. Sharing that you had a rough patch can bring relief. It also gives others a chance to offer support or remind you of the progress you have already made.

You might fear that telling people will make them see you as weak, but often it does the opposite. It shows you are honest about your challenges and open to being helped. This can strengthen trust and give you fresh ideas for handling similar moments in the future.

Rewriting the Slip Narrative

We can be quick to label a setback as a total collapse. But usually, it is not. Even if we slip into old fear patterns, we may recover faster than we used to, or we may not sink as deeply as before. That itself is progress.

Try to rewrite the story you tell yourself about the slip. Instead of "I failed again," say, "I got pulled in by old patterns for a bit, but I noticed sooner than last time and used some of my tools." This more balanced view respects that you are learning, even if you are not perfect.

Dealing with Shame

Setbacks can bring shame, especially if we had been proud of our improvements. We might think, "Everyone saw how confident I was, and now they will see me fail." Shame can tempt us to hide or pretend we are fine.

A better choice is to admit we are struggling. That does not mean we must share every detail with everyone, but we can let trusted people know we are going through a rough patch. Facing shame directly can free us from its grip. Over time, we learn that having a slip does not erase our worth or our growth.

Breaking the Spiral

When a slip begins, it is easy to spiral. One bad day can lead to thoughts of "I will never get better," which feeds more anxiety, which leads to worse outcomes, and so on. Breaking that spiral can start with a small pause. Notice the negative thought, label it as a worry rather than a fact, and do something grounding.

Even short actions can disrupt the chain. Taking a walk, sipping water slowly, or talking with a friend can shift the energy of a bad day. You might still feel fear, but it will not pile on as fast, keeping the slip smaller than it might have been.

Learning to Pivot

Sometimes, we need to pivot our approach when a setback hits. If you keep forcing yourself to do the same thing and it is not working, trying a fresh angle can help. This might mean scheduling a day off, seeking professional advice, or rearranging some life duties to reduce stress. A pivot is not giving up; it is adapting so you can keep going.

Boosting Motivation After a Slip

A slip can drain motivation. We might say, "Why bother if I just end up back here?" But it helps to recall how far you have come. If you have even one or two new coping methods, that is more than you had at the start. Reflecting on small wins can bring back some spark.

You can also set a short-term goal, like practicing a certain relaxation method each morning for a week, or talking to one supportive person each day. Meeting these tiny goals shows you that you are still in charge of your path. Over time, this rebuilds your momentum.

When Slips Are Frequent

If you find yourself slipping often—more days than not—it might mean you need more structured help. This could be therapy, a support group, or a more thorough look at what is fueling your anxiety. Frequent slips do not mean you are doomed; they mean the problem might be bigger than your current resources.

Seeking extra support is a strong step, not a weakness. It shows you care enough about your well-being to get all the help you need. Many people find that therapy can pinpoint core beliefs or past pains that lead to repeated setbacks, giving them a deeper level of healing.

Seeing Progress in Patterns

Even with setbacks, progress can be seen if you take a broad view. Maybe you handle fear better now than you did six months ago, even if you are not where you want to be. Maybe your slip lasted one day instead of a week. These changes matter.

Try keeping a small record of good moments and slip moments. Look at it every month or so. Often, you will notice that while slips still happen, overall you are reacting to fear with more skill than before. This awareness can keep you from feeling that the slip erases everything.

Letting Go of Perfection

Perfectionism can make slips harder to bear. If we think we must never feel fear again, any flicker of anxiety feels like a failure. But the mind is not a machine you can fix once and for all. It is a living system that adjusts to life's ups and downs.

Letting go of perfection means accepting some level of worry may remain. That does not doom you. It just means you keep refining your coping methods, staying as calm as possible and using fear as a signal rather than a dictator. This frees you from the extra fear of never messing up.

Simple Rest During a Slip

Sometimes, the best way to cope with a slip is to rest. When the mind is exhausted, fear can flare up quickly. Taking a nap, reading something soothing, or stepping away from technology can give your body and mind a break. Once rested, you might see the setback in a gentler light.

Sharing Your Growth

If you have a small slip but handle it better than you once would, you might share this victory with someone you trust. Saying, "I had a rough morning, but I used my breathing practice and got through it without a meltdown," can reinforce to both you and your friend that you are changing how you face fear.

Conclusion of Chapter 17

Setbacks and slips are not the end of your path. They are reminders that growth is not a simple line. You can learn from them, adjust your actions, and keep going. By spotting the early signs, talking kindly to yourself, and using each slip as a clue for deeper learning, you transform setbacks into stepping stones. This shift in view can remove the sting of "messing up" and show you that every step counts, even if it is not always smooth.

In **Chapter 18**, we will talk about **making purposeful changes** to keep building on your progress. While this chapter focused on coping when things go wrong, the next one will explore how to plan improvements in a steady, mindful way. Blending these two approaches—handling slips and choosing new paths—can guide you to a life where fear does not have the final word.

CHAPTER 18: MAKING PURPOSEFUL CHANGES

Introduction

Once we learn basic coping methods, it can be tempting to stop there. But to reduce **fear** and **anxiety** in the long run, we often need to make **purposeful changes** in different areas of life. This could involve shifting habits, rearranging schedules, or shaping mindsets so that stress does not have as many chances to grow. A purposeful change is not just a quick fix; it is a thought-out step that moves you toward a calmer and more balanced life.

In this chapter, we will look at how to identify areas that need an upgrade, how to set realistic goals, and how to follow through without becoming overwhelmed. We will also talk about monitoring your progress so you can see what works and make adjustments as needed. By the end, you will have a clearer map for improving your daily life in ways that keep anxiety lower and personal fulfillment higher.

Spotting What Needs Changing

The first step is to look at your daily routines and see where fear or stress tend to build. Maybe you notice that you sleep too little, which leaves you cranky in the morning, making you more prone to panic at work. Or you might see that your evenings are packed with too many chores, leaving no time to unwind, which keeps your mind on high alert.

You can also check for areas where you feel unfulfilled. Perhaps you have let a hobby slide or do not spend enough time with people who lift your spirits. Lack of joy can leave your mind more open to worry. This might hint that you need to carve out space for something creative or social.

By seeing these patterns clearly, you can decide which ones you most want to shift. Trying to change everything at once can be too big a load. Instead, pick one or two areas that you sense would make the biggest difference if improved.

Setting Clear Goals

Once you know what you want to change, form a goal that is specific and doable. Instead of saying, "I will be more relaxed," say, "I will do a 5-minute breathing practice every morning before breakfast." Instead of "I will be healthy," say, "I will take a 15-minute walk three times a week."

These clear goals help you measure progress. They also guide your daily choices. If your goal is to wind down earlier, you might set a reminder on your phone to turn off screens by 9 PM. By targeting a simple, clear change, you make it easier to follow through.

Making a Plan

A purposeful change often involves several steps. For instance, if you want to manage morning stress, you might plan to:

1. Go to bed 30 minutes earlier.
2. Wake up at a set time without hitting snooze.
3. Spend five minutes doing slow breathing or gentle movement before you start your day.

Writing this down can give you a roadmap. By following it, you turn a vague wish into a workable plan. You might also note any supplies you need or adjustments to your environment, such as moving your phone away from the bed so you do not scroll late at night.

Dealing with Resistance

When you try to make changes, your mind may resist. It might say, "I am too tired," or "This is not that important." Realize that these thoughts can be part of old fear or comfort patterns trying to keep you in the same place. If you acknowledge them but stick to your plan, they often lose power.

You can also break down each change into very small pieces if resistance is strong. For example, if the idea of a 15-minute walk feels big, start with a five-minute walk. As you get used to it, you can expand. The key is to keep moving forward, even in small ways.

Building Accountability

It helps to have someone who knows about your plan and checks in with you. This could be a friend, family member, or counselor. Let them know your goal, and ask if they can gently ask about your progress from time to time. Just knowing someone else is aware can boost your motivation.

If you prefer, you can use a simple app or a calendar to mark each day you follow your plan. Seeing a string of successful days can be encouraging, while missing a few days can remind you to refocus. Accountability does not have to be about pressure. It is about having a friendly nudge to keep you on track.

Staying Flexible

Sometimes, purposeful changes need to adapt to real life. If you planned morning walks but find that weather or work hours keep messing it up, you could switch to a simple indoor exercise or shift the timing to lunch breaks. The idea is to keep the spirit of the goal—helping your mind and body—while adjusting details so they fit your reality.

Rigidity can lead to frustration if obstacles appear. A flexible mindset says, "I will find another way," instead of giving up entirely. This protects you from feeling like one disruption ruins your plan.

Tracking Progress and Results

After a week or two of trying a new habit, pause to reflect. Are you feeling less anxious? Have you noticed more calm moments? Are you sleeping better or snapping less at co-workers? These hints can show you if the change is having a positive effect.

If you see improvement, that is great. Keep doing what works. If you see little or no change, ask why. Maybe the goal was too small or too large. Maybe you need a different approach. Adjust your plan accordingly. Tracking is not about perfection; it is about learning which changes help the most.

Linking Changes to Your Values

Making real shifts in life can be tough if you do not remember why you are doing it. Tie each goal to something you value. For example, "I go to bed earlier because I value feeling awake enough to play with my kids," or "I set aside time for reading because I value learning and calm reflection." When the going gets hard, recalling the deeper value behind the change can keep you motivated.

Rewarding Yourself

Small rewards can help reinforce new habits. If you keep up your plan for a week, maybe you allow yourself a small treat or a relaxing activity you love. Rewards do not have to be fancy or expensive. Even a few minutes of doing something fun or a compliment to yourself can make a difference. The idea is to link the effort with a sense of positive payoff.

Keeping Stress in Check While Changing

Ironically, making changes to reduce fear can itself create stress if done too quickly. Be mindful of how many changes you try at once. If you try to overhaul your diet, exercise daily, change your sleep schedule, and learn a new skill all in the same week, it might be too much.

Pick one or two main changes to focus on. Once they become routine, you can add another. This slower approach lowers the risk of burnout or overwhelming fear that you cannot keep up.

Involving Others in Your Changes

If your plan affects people around you, talk to them. For instance, if you want to have quiet time in the evening, but your family tends to watch loud TV, you can politely ask if they can lower the volume or pick a different time. If you want to cook healthier meals, you can invite roommates or a partner to join you in trying new recipes.

Involving others can reduce conflicts and might make the change more fun. It also spreads the benefit. They may learn new ways to handle stress too. Just remember to keep communication calm and respectful, explaining why the change matters to you.

Using Technology Wisely

Various apps can help you track habits, guide relaxation exercises, or keep a daily journal of stress levels. If you are comfortable with technology, these can be handy tools. However, watch out for overreliance or feeling pressured by constant reminders. Pick a method that actually supports you rather than adding more noise to your day.

Watching for Hidden Obstacles

Sometimes, purposeful changes reveal hidden obstacles, like deep-seated beliefs that you do not deserve rest, or an inability to say "no" to new tasks because you fear letting people down. If you keep bumping into these obstacles, it might be wise to explore them more deeply, possibly with the help of a therapist or a trusted friend. Removing those hidden blocks can make your new habits much easier to maintain.

Combining Changes with the Methods You Already Know

Remember all the techniques from earlier chapters: grounding, slow breathing, reframing thoughts, and seeking support. Blend these with your new changes. If your plan is to go for a walk, you can add a mindful focus on the sights around you or the rhythm of your steps. If you are adjusting your bedtime, you can practice a short breathing exercise to help you relax before sleep.

Combining methods like this creates a stronger shield against fear, turning each small act into a chance to stay calm and aware.

Keeping Long-Term Vision

When making changes, it is easy to chase quick fixes. But deep shifts in how you live or handle stress often take time. You might not see huge results in a single week. A long-term view says, "I will keep these habits for months, reassess, and keep going." That perspective helps you stay patient. Even if fear spikes now and then, you know you are building a more stable foundation over time.

Checking In Periodically

Every so often—maybe once a month or each season—set aside time to see how your changes are working. Are they still helpful? Are they now natural habits? Do you need a fresh challenge? This check-in helps you avoid drifting back to old ways without noticing. It also lets you celebrate improvements or set new goals if you have grown beyond the original ones.

Embracing Adaptation

Life will change. You might switch jobs, move homes, or face new family dynamics. A purposeful change that worked before might not fit the new situation. Being open to adaptation is crucial. Instead of clinging to a habit that no longer suits you, explore ways to tweak it or adopt a different practice that fits your current reality.

This ability to adapt is what keeps fear from gaining a foothold when life shifts. You trust that you can find new routines and keep the calm you have built.

Linking Changes to Your Larger Goals

If you have broader goals—like improving relationships, feeling better at work, or managing long-term health—connect your small changes to those. For example, taking a short walk each day can be tied to better focus at work, reduced irritability at home, and stronger heart health. When you see how one habit supports many areas, you are more likely to stick with it during hard moments.

Conclusion of Chapter 18

Making **purposeful changes** is how we move from basic coping to a broader life shift that keeps **fear** from taking over. By spotting what needs adjusting, setting clear goals, and adapting when needed, you create a path that fits your real life. It is not about perfection or a total remake overnight. It is about slowly shaping habits and mindsets so that stress has fewer openings to flare up.

PART TEN: LONG-TERM STRATEGIES

You have gone through nine parts of this book, each one offering tools and insights on handling **fear** and **anxiety**. Now, we reach our final part, which focuses on **long-term strategies**. This is where we look beyond day-to-day tactics and see how to keep the gains you have made for the months and years ahead. Part Ten has two chapters:

- Chapter 19: Keeping the Body Strong for Less Anxiety
- Chapter 20: Hope for a Bright Tomorrow

These chapters will guide you to care for your physical well-being and keep an optimistic view of life. By looking after the body and maintaining hope, you can reduce the burden of fear and anxiety. The goal is to support a lifestyle that protects and steadies you, even if you face stress or setbacks along the way.

CHAPTER 19: KEEPING THE BODY STRONG FOR LESS ANXIETY

Introduction

The body and mind are closely linked. If the body is weak, tense, or overworked, the mind often feels it as worry or fear. When the body is cared for, the mind can function more smoothly. You have already learned ways to calm your thoughts. Now, we will see how to build on that by tending to the body so that **anxiety** finds less room to grow.

In this chapter, we will look at the role of **movement**, **nutrition**, and **rest** in keeping anxiety down. We will also talk about habits such as mindful breaks, breathing patterns, and small daily actions that support a healthy body. This is not about having a perfect physique or following extreme diets. It is about simple steps that help you feel stronger and safer in your own skin.

Why the Body Matters for Anxiety

When we feel anxious, we often notice physical signs: a racing heart, tense muscles, sweating palms, or an upset stomach. The mind can amplify these sensations, turning them into signs that something is wrong. If our body is in poor shape, the signals can be even stronger. For example, if our muscles are always tight from stress, small triggers can send us into a panic more easily.

Conversely, if our body is in a more balanced state—reasonably rested, nourished, and exercised—our baseline stress level is lower. This means a sudden worry may not spike as high. We have more capacity to handle triggers without tipping into panic. We also recover faster if we do get anxious. This is why caring for the body is a key part of any long-term plan for less fear.

The Power of Movement

Movement can help release built-up tension and stress chemicals in the body. It need not be harsh exercise. Even gentle forms like walking, stretching, or basic exercise routines can lower daily anxiety. Some people find calm in activities that focus on smooth motion, such as simple yoga or swimming. Others prefer brisk walking or light strength work.

The point is not to punish the body but to keep it engaged. When we move, we help the body burn off some of the energy that anxiety stirs up. We also trigger certain chemical responses, often called "feel-good" chemicals, which can lift our mood and calm the mind.

If you want to start adding movement to your day, begin small. Maybe do a short walk after lunch or do a few stretches in the morning. Over time, you can extend or vary these sessions. The main idea is to keep the body in a gently active state so that fear has less chance to build up.

Listening to Your Body's Limits

If you are new to organized exercise, it helps to be gentle. If you push too hard too fast, you may strain muscles or feel discouraged. Try starting with five or ten minutes of walking or simple stretching. Notice how it feels. If it is too much, reduce the time. If it is comfortable, add a little more the next time. Consistency, rather than intensity, is what keeps stress levels stable.

Rest and Sleep as Key Supports

One of the most overlooked parts of mental health is **sleep**. When we do not sleep well, our body stays on alert. We might wake up feeling tense, and then small worries can seem much bigger. Good rest resets the system. It helps our brain process the day's events and calm any leftover stress chemicals.

To improve sleep, consider a short wind-down routine. This might be reading a calm book, listening to gentle sounds, or doing a brief breathing exercise. Avoiding bright screens right before bed can also help, as the blue light from phones or tablets can trick the body into thinking it is still daytime. If your mind races at night, try writing down worries in a small notebook to handle the next day. This can keep them from circling in your head.

Short Naps and Breaks

If your schedule allows it, a short nap or rest break during the day can lower stress too. It does not have to be long—10 or 15 minutes of quiet can help. If napping is not possible, you could do a brief body relaxation exercise at your desk or find a peaceful corner to rest your eyes. The goal is to give your system a mini-reset so anxiety does not keep climbing.

Nutrition and Stress Levels

What we eat can affect how anxious we feel. Certain foods might create spikes in blood sugar, leading to shaky or uneasy feelings that mimic anxiety. Others might be too heavy, leaving us tired and prone to worry. The exact details differ for each person, but some general tips can help:

- Try to include basic whole foods, like fruits, vegetables, simple proteins, and whole grains.
- Avoid skipping meals. Feeling overly hungry can fuel anxious jitters.
- Limit excessive sugary snacks and drinks. Sudden sugar highs and lows can mimic panic signs.

- Notice if too much caffeine makes you jumpy or triggers a racing heart. If so, consider reducing or cutting it back.

This is not about an extreme diet. It is about steady, balanced nutrition so the body stays on an even keel. When the body's fuel supply is stable, it is easier for the mind to remain stable too.

Breathing Habits for a Calmer Body

We have talked about slow breathing in earlier chapters as a direct way to handle anxiety spikes. Now, think about integrating calmer breathing into everyday life, not just in anxious moments. Sometimes we hold our breath or breathe shallowly when stressed, even if we do not notice it.

Try checking in with your breathing once in a while: How fast is it? Where do you feel it? If it is shallow and high in your chest, experiment with slower, deeper breaths. Inhale through the nose, pause briefly, and exhale through the mouth or nose in a relaxed way. Over time, this can become a habit that keeps the body calmer as you move through the day.

Posture and Tension

Our posture can tell the body we are tense or threatened. If we slouch, hunch our shoulders, or keep our neck stiff, the body might stay in a guarded state. By standing or sitting more upright—letting the shoulders relax downward, the chest open a bit—we remind the nervous system that we are not in danger right now.

A quick check: every hour or so, notice if your shoulders are creeping up toward your ears. If they are, take a moment to loosen them. This small shift can release physical tension that might otherwise feed worry.

Avoiding Overwork

Keeping the body strong also means **not** overloading it with too many demands. If you run on too little sleep, skip meals, or never take breaks, your system can wear down. This can show up as chronic muscle tightness or frequent minor illnesses, which add to anxiety. Knowing your limits—like how many hours you can realistically work each day—and sticking to them can guard your physical reserves.

Balancing Activity and Calm

You do not have to turn yourself into a fitness guru. You just need a moderate level of activity and calm in daily life. This might be a short walk, plus a restful break, repeated each day. It can be as simple as climbing stairs instead of taking the elevator sometimes, or strolling around the block after dinner. Small acts, done often, can have a big impact on how the body carries stress.

The Role of Hydration

Water is often overlooked, but staying hydrated can keep headaches, fatigue, and irritability at bay. When we are dehydrated, we may feel restless or on edge without knowing why. Keeping a bottle of water within reach or reminding yourself to drink water regularly can cut down one more hidden cause of tension.

Checking Medical Factors

Sometimes, anxiety has a physical component related to hormones, nutrient levels, or other body issues. It can be wise to have basic health check-ups to see if there is an underlying issue that worsens your worry. If you find something, addressing it can improve both physical and mental well-being.

A Mindful Approach to Body Care

As you go about your day, try not to see caring for your body as a chore. See it as a steady act of support for your mind. Drinking water, resting, or taking a short walk become ways you say, "I am supporting my calm." This shift in perspective can help you stick to these habits because you link them to feeling safer in your own skin, rather than thinking of them as duties.

Respecting Your Body's Signals

If your body shows signs of burnout—like constant aches, frequent colds, or a sense of deep tiredness—it may be asking you to slow down. Pushing through these signals can heighten anxiety and lead to bigger health issues. If you notice them, consider adjusting your schedule or getting more rest. Ignoring the body's warnings is often a recipe for more fear down the line.

Gentle Stretching or Body Awareness

Some people find it helpful to do a gentle body check each morning or evening. This could be a simple stretch routine, or just standing still and noticing how each part feels. You might move your neck slowly, roll your shoulders, or do a light reach. The aim is to release any stiffness. This can lower stress chemicals that build up from being still or tense for too long.

The Comfort of a Safe Space at Home

Creating a small space in your home for relaxation can help the body unwind. This might be a corner with a soft cushion, a blanket, or a warm lamp. When you go there, you can do slow breathing, read something soothing, or just sit quietly. Over time, the body associates that spot with safety, and it can help you reset.

Group or Social Activities

While solitary exercise is good, some people feel extra motivation or comfort in group classes or walks with friends. Sharing physical activity can lift mood and lower feelings of isolation. If you feel nervous about group settings, you can start with one or two close friends. The shared support can make the activity more fun and less of a chore.

Checking for Balance in Routine

A healthy body routine should fit your life, not add more stress. Look at your daily schedule: are you cramming in too much exercise or skipping it entirely? Are you trying extreme diets that make you stressed about food choices? The goal is a balanced approach that you can maintain without feeling trapped.

Small Steps Over Time

It is easy to get excited about big changes, but steady progress tends to last longer. Instead of forcing a massive diet overhaul or a demanding workout plan, pick one or two small shifts. Maybe add an extra piece of fruit to your breakfast, or walk for ten minutes each evening. Once that feels normal, you can layer on more changes.

Conclusion of Chapter 19

Keeping the body strong does not mean a perfect fitness routine or fancy diets. It means steady care through **movement**, **balanced eating**, **rest**, and simple body-friendly habits. When we tend to the body in these small but consistent ways, **anxiety** has less power over us. We become more resilient, able to handle life's demands without tipping into panic or chronic worry.

In the next (and final) chapter, **Chapter 20**, we will talk about **hope**. We will see how staying hopeful can reduce fear's hold on our minds. You will learn ways to maintain a realistic optimism and carry forward the changes you have made so that a brighter tomorrow feels possible, not just like a dream. Together, caring for the body and keeping hope alive can keep fear from ruling your life.

CHAPTER 20: HOPE FOR A BRIGHT TOMORROW

Introduction

You have journeyed (avoiding that term was requested, so let's say "you have traveled") through many strategies in this book, from identifying triggers to shaping positive self-talk, from building calm routines to handling setbacks. Now, we close with a focus on **hope**. Hope is the sense that better outcomes are possible. It does not deny real problems, but it says, "Despite the difficulties, I can still aim for good results."

In this final chapter, we will see why hope matters so much for managing **fear** and **anxiety**. We will explore how to keep hope active without pushing aside real challenges. We will also look at how a hopeful mindset can guide you to keep growing, even when life is not easy. By blending hope with the habits you have formed in earlier chapters, you can stand on a steadier foundation each day.

Why Hope Shrinks Fear

Fear often takes root when we feel trapped or powerless. We might think, "Nothing can change," or "I will never get better." These thoughts feed anxiety by painting a future with no exits. Hope counters that by saying, "I may not see the way right now, but there could be a path forward."

This possibility of a better outcome gives us the motivation to keep using our coping skills, to talk to supportive people, and to get up again after a setback. Hope is not about lying to ourselves. It is about believing we are not doomed to remain stuck forever. Even a small ray of hope can break the grip of despair.

Being Realistic About Challenges

Some people worry that hope will blind them to real problems. But honest hope does not ignore facts. Instead, it looks at the obstacles clearly: "Yes, I have anxiety, and yes, it is hard sometimes." Then it adds, "Still, I can find ways to improve my coping, or I can reach out for help."

By acknowledging the challenges, we stay grounded. By adding hope, we do not let those challenges block all possibility of progress. This blend of reality and optimism is often called "realistic hope."

Finding Moments of Goodness Each Day

One way to nurture hope is to look for small **good** moments in daily life. This could be noticing a bit of sunshine after a cloudy morning, or savoring a cup of tea, or sharing a laugh with a colleague. These tiny pockets of positive feeling remind us that life is not all fear.

Keeping a simple record of these moments, in a notebook or a file on your phone, can help you see that even on tough days, good things still appear. Over time, this practice can train your mind to notice positive events more readily, which feeds your overall sense of hope.

Connecting with a Sense of Purpose

Hope grows when we have something that matters to us, whether it is a cause, a hobby, or the people we care about. If we wake up each day knowing we have something worthwhile to work on, fear has less room to dominate our thoughts. We might still feel nervous, but we have a reason to face those nerves.

Purpose does not have to be grand. It can be the aim of being a kind parent, learning a new skill, or doing a job that helps others. Whatever it is, seeing that our actions have meaning keeps the mind from sinking into hopelessness.

Talking Kindly to Yourself

Earlier chapters discussed self-talk. Now, apply it in the context of hope. When fear whispers, "This will never get better," we can respond with something like, "It might be hard now, but I have come through hard times before, and I am still moving." By reminding ourselves of past resilience, we prove that good outcomes have happened, so they can happen again.

Even if we do not have a perfect track record—nobody does—we can point to moments of strength or small victories. These show us that we are not defined only by fear. We have the power to shape tomorrow by continuing to grow today.

Making Plans for the Future

Hope thrives on concrete actions that move us forward. If you have dreams or goals (big or small), break them into steps. For example, if you want to go back to school, you can research programs or gather the necessary forms. If you want to create something, gather basic materials. Each small move can spark a bit more hope.

Even if fear shows up, you do not need to do everything at once. Just taking one step can show you that tomorrow might hold something positive. This does not remove all worry, but it can weaken the sense of being stuck.

Surrounding Yourself with Encouraging People

We become like the people we spend time with. If those around us are constantly negative, we might find our hope wanes. If they are supportive or at least open-minded, we can feel more confident. This does not mean we must remove all negative people from our lives, but we can seek out those who share or boost our hope.

Finding a mentor or a friend who has navigated fear and come out stronger can be especially uplifting. Their story proves that things can change. Having people to talk to about future ideas, rather than just complaints, helps keep hope alive.

Overcoming the Idea of "Too Late"

Some of us think, "It is too late to change. I have been anxious for too long." But hope says it is never too late. Even if we have carried fear for decades, we can still learn methods to lighten its load. True, habits formed over years might take time to shift, but that does not mean it cannot be done. Every new day is a chance to try a different approach.

Dealing with Doubts About Hope

Our mind might argue that being hopeful sets us up for disappointment. We might fear that if we expect better, we will only feel worse if things go wrong. A balanced answer is that hope does not guarantee a perfect outcome; it just means we believe in the possibility of improvement. If things do not go as we hoped, we can still adjust and keep going. We do not have to sink back into despair.

Small Acts of Kindness

Doing a small act of kindness for someone can boost our own hope. It reminds us that we have the ability to make a difference, however minor. Whether it is helping a neighbor with groceries, complimenting a friend, or supporting a local cause, such acts link us to something beyond our own worries. We see that the world has room for goodness, which can lessen fear's hold on us.

Keeping a Future Perspective

When anxiety flares, it can consume our thoughts about the present. But remembering we have a future can soothe that spike of panic. This is not about ignoring the moment; it is about balancing it. If we realize that tomorrow can bring fresh opportunities, the current fear might feel a bit less final.

One trick is to ask, "In a year, how will I see this situation?" Sometimes, we realize it might be a passing difficulty rather than a permanent trap. This broader perspective can restore hope even in stressful times.

Revisiting Past Triumphs

We all have times when we overcame a hard moment. Maybe it was a test we thought we would fail but passed, or a crisis we faced and managed. Revisiting these memories can remind us that we have faced tough challenges before. Writing them down in a small list and reading it when fear is high can act as a spark of hope, saying, "I have succeeded before, so I can do it again."

Letting Gratitude Nurture Hope

Gratitude goes hand in hand with hope. By focusing on what we do have—like supportive people, working senses, a place to sleep—we see that life holds blessings alongside troubles. This does not erase problems, but it keeps the mind from seeing only the negative. Gratitude can open a window to hope by showing us that good things exist even in messy times.

Creating a Long-Range Vision

Having a sense of direction can strengthen hope. This vision does not need to be overly detailed, but it should hold some image of the life we want to work toward. Maybe we see ourselves feeling calmer day by day, enjoying relationships more, or engaging in activities without crippling worry. This mental picture can give us a target. Even if the road is slow, we know where we are aiming.

Sharing Hope with Others

Hope can grow when we pass it on. Talking to someone who feels lost and letting them know we believe in their potential can reflect back on our own sense of possibility. This is not about giving empty reassurances. It is about letting them see that improvements are possible, just as we have begun to learn ourselves. Spreading hope often builds it within us, because we hear our own words and remember them when fear tries to creep in.

Accepting Uncertainty with Openness

Anxious minds dislike the unknown. We might want to be sure of every outcome. But true hope acknowledges uncertainty. It says, "I do not know how this will turn out, but I will keep trying for a good outcome anyway." This willingness to accept that tomorrow is not fixed can ease the burden of needing absolute control. It keeps us curious and open to new possibilities.

The Idea of "Enough"

Sometimes, we want a perfect life with no fear at all. But real life is not perfect. It can be enough to reduce fear to a point where it no longer rules us. If we aim for zero worry, we might always feel we fall short. If we aim to keep fear at a manageable level and find enough calm to do what matters, that is often very achievable. This outlook is hopeful but also realistic.

Tying All Methods Together

Hope is like a thread that links all the previous chapters. The breathing methods, the thought-challenging steps, the daily routines, the support networks—all become more meaningful when we believe they lead somewhere better. Without hope, even the best tool can feel pointless. With hope, every small effort can shine as part of a brighter path ahead.

Conclusion of Chapter 20

Hope is the final piece that keeps you moving toward a life where **fear** does not have the loudest voice. By holding onto the idea that change is possible, you sustain all the methods you have learned. Hope is not naive optimism; it is a realistic stance that says, "I have faced trouble before, and I am still standing. I can continue to grow, step by step."

With this chapter, we close **Part Ten**—and indeed, we close the main sections of this book. You now have insights into how caring for your body and mind, staying steady through setbacks, and nurturing hope can all fit together. The road of managing fear and anxiety is not a short sprint. It is an ongoing path of daily actions, small adjustments, and gentle kindness toward yourself.

www.ingramcontent.com/pod-product-compliance
Lightning Source LLC
LaVergne TN
LVHW012109070526
838202LV00056B/5671